Game Economy Design

This book provides a comprehensive overview of game economy design. It begins with a high-level overview, then utilizes subsequent chapters to break this down into finer details, showing methods to approach the various problems and challenges involved in creating an intricate game economy and metagame experience. The content of the book extends to associated and related fields such as monetization and live operations.

The book contains step-by-step processes with best practices and examples, with content written from an empirical standpoint. The reader will gain insights into the components that form a game economy, how these components are utilized to shape a metagame experience and how monetization is integrated into this. The content will consider the work economy designers undertake during development through to postlaunch live operations.

The book will appeal to all game design professionals and students of game design that wish to gain a deeper understanding of how to develop game economies.

Game Economy Design
Metagame, Monetization and Live Operations

Charlie Czerkawski

CRC Press
Taylor & Francis Group
Boca Raton London New York

CRC Press is an imprint of the
Taylor & Francis Group, an **informa** business

Designed cover image: Matt Zanetti

First edition published 2025
by CRC Press
2385 NW Executive Center Drive, Suite 320, Boca Raton FL 33431

and by CRC Press
4 Park Square, Milton Park, Abingdon, Oxon, OX14 4RN

CRC Press is an imprint of Taylor & Francis Group, LLC

© 2025 Charlie Czerkawski

ISBN: 9781032479927 (hbk)
ISBN: 9781032479903 (pbk)
ISBN: 9781003386865 (ebk)

DOI: 10.1201/9781003386865

Typeset in Adobe Caslon Pro
by KnowledgeWorks Global Ltd.

Contents

Foreword

I started my career in video games in 1996 as a programmer and at that time we did basic game experiences delivered on CD-ROM through retail stores. You did one game and best of cases it was appreciated so you could do a sequel. Later, in 2002, when I was the Head of Studio at DICE Stockholm our team delivered Battlefield 1942 and I started to realize that the game could have such a much longer lifetime and relationship with the customer. It wasn't just about "release and forget" your game but we shipped several downloadable contents (DLC's) and modding tools and supported the community to create their own experiences. When downloading games through Steam and other similar stores became the dominating way of distribution it opened up so many more ways of exploring add-on sales to games. In my roles at Paradox Interactive and later as CEO of Starbreeze we worked with games that had years of ongoing service to our customers in the form of both free upgrades and paid DLC of all kinds of formats. Personally I have always liked this model also as a consumer of games because somebody out there is making sure you get value for your bucks over time.

When I had the pleasure of working with Charlie at Starbreeze we talked about the importance of offering this kind of added content in such a way that it truly is a positive experience for the gamer and how easy it is to make mistakes. One of the reasons that mistakes are easily done is that it is a fairly new method in the greater scheme of things, especially when, as Charlie writes about in this book, offering it within the game itself.

You will get a great introduction to how to build your in-game economy and store through practical and usable examples. I want to point out that this is not only reading for the person responsible for the in-game store but is extremely valuable information for a lot more disciplines like Producers, Game Designers and UI-experts to just name a few. When implementing this in your game you will also see how important it is to have people from various backgrounds to validate that this is something that adheres to the large group of gamers out there. Live operations and treating games as an ongoing service are clearly the future of the game industry and the examples are plentiful, both good ones and bad ones. Games are also products that continuously develop in the way they are constructed, sold and distributed, marketed and monetized. Getting a fundamental understanding for in-game sales will help you as a reader to be ready for the future iterations in this field.

Charlie has through his passion for this area, deep knowledge in mathematics and experience from the game industry created a distillation of his body of work that adds to the common knowledge base for all of us in the game industry and that helps us all make better experiences for our customers. This will help our industry to continue to develop and become better and I can encourage you as a reader of this book to follow Charlie's great example and share your knowledge with others and help us all deliver better game experiences.

I'm most grateful to Charlie for taking the time and efforts to write this book, I know his work will help myself and others to create better games and ensure happier gamers all around the world.

Tobias Sjögren

Acknowledgments

This book would never have come about without the help and support of certain individuals. I would like to give a huge thank-you to Heikki Joas, by whom I was fortunate enough to be coached, while working in the Czech Republic. This was when I learned a colossal amount about game economy and monetization design in a relatively short space of time.

I would like to thank my friend and past business partner Matt Zanetti for his art skills used in creating the front cover image, along with the diagrams found within the book. Mention must also be made of my other friends and business partners at Guerilla Tea in Dundee, Scotland: Alex Zeitler and Mark Hastings. Running a game development company for seven years was a steep but worthwhile learning curve for all of us.

Thanks must go to all at CRC Press for giving me the opportunity to write this book, to C.L. Czerkawska for editing assistance and, finally, to the late Dr. Tommy Whitelaw of Glasgow University, who succeeded in passing on his love of mathematics to all his students throughout 50 years of teaching and advising.

Charlie Czerkawski, Sweden, 2024

Author Biography

Charlie Czerkawski is a game economy and monetization design expert, who has been developing games professionally for over 15 years. He is a graduate of Glasgow University, having majored in mathematics, and went on to attain a postgraduate MProf in Video Games Development at Abertay University in Dundee. He was the co-founder of Scottish independent development studio Guerilla Tea, which operated from 2011 to 2017.

He has worked as a game economy designer, monetization manager and team lead, developing games for PC, Console and Mobile. His career has taken him around Europe, working on titles including Shadowgun Legends, PAYDAY 3 and Exoborne. He was recognized in Develop magazine's 30 under 30 for 2016.

When not making games, he is a keen sportsperson, having attained a shodan black belt in Shotokai karate, while also focussing on competitive rowing, competing in the 2024 World Indoor Rowing Championships. He also has a passion for adventure, and takes any opportunity he can to see and explore the world.

INTRODUCTION

Video games are a unique entertainment medium. They have seen an unprecedented evolution over the years, in tandem with increasingly powerful hardware. The interactive nature of video games sets them apart from other entertainment media, and it is this element that drives the sheer breadth of user experiences available on the market.

Over the years, genres of games have evolved and expanded, with design innovations creating new ways for players to play. A key factor in driving innovation is advancement in technology. The concept of game economy and monetization has developed over the years in tandem with this technological advancement.

As the general complexity of games has increased, so has the need for features that surround the core gameplay, known as metagame features. These ultimately add layers of depth to the overall player experience and support long-term player engagement.

The rise of mobile gaming has led to the widespread adoption of the free-to-play business model, which has given birth to new game design approaches, with their focus on player retention and monetization methods integrated into the design from the ground up.

With the power of the modern-day internet, the period of time after the initial launch of a game has become more important than it ever was for developers, who can now support titles with regular updates. This has, in turn, given rise to the Games-as-a-Service delivery model, whereby games become long term, evolving products with new fixes, features and content.

Game economy, monetization and live operations have their roots within these innovations.

Who Is This Book for?

Game economy design can be considered to be a relatively specialized discipline within the games industry, and naturally this book is

DOI: 10.1201/9781003386865-1

primarily aimed at those who have a strong interest in this field. With this in mind, I have written the book for an intended target audience of either game development students or those within the industry at the early stages of their careers.

Game design as a whole is highly collaborative, and game designers who are concerned with other aspects of the player's experience will inevitably find themselves working closely with game economy designers, so there are insights within the book which will be of interest to other specializations within game design.

You, as a Person

One of my key objectives when writing this book was to try to avoid making too many assumptions. Naturally, there is a base level of video game knowledge that is taken for granted. I expect that the reader has the ability to think analytically about games, and that this reader works from the principle that games are a business, and must make money to be sustainable.

As far as technical proficiency with specific software is concerned, this only extends to the ability to use word processing software and spreadsheets. For game economy design, becoming familiar with spreadsheet software is of utmost importance. While I will cover the fundamental knowledge of spreadsheet software, this book does not include extensive spreadsheet tutorials. This information is more efficiently sourced on the internet. Spreadsheet software typically includes a plethora of functionality, and for game economy design you will realistically only need to use a proportion of this. I generally write from the principle that you can work with basic spreadsheet functions and will quickly Google unknown aspects while working to improve your skills.

Aspects of mathematics underpin many parts of game development, in particular game economy design. The book has a section covering mathematical skills and some loose applications within design. Mathematics is an imagined world in itself and requires an extremely abstract way of thinking. I have been conscientious about walking through the very basics of math and not taking for granted that the reader will necessarily be comfortable with the fundamentals of elementary algebra, which includes the skill of manipulating variables within equations.

Game economy and monetization design is a *problem-solving role*. For any project, there is a limited time and budget and, consequently, limited development resources. Your job as a designer is to find optimal solutions to design problems within these constraints. You will often hear experienced designers talking about the problems they faced and how they solved them. While it is impractical, if not impossible, to teach the abstract idea of generic problem solving, habits can be developed to aid the cause. When faced with a problem, there are many things you can do to, at the very least, move closer to a solution. It helps to stop and take a step back and think about the problem from different angles. While seeking help from a co-worker should never be actively discouraged, it is highly beneficial to dedicate some time to trying to come up with a solution yourself. Many problems pertaining to software and game development have solutions posted online, and re-applying the solution to a similar problem is a very viable approach. Having the ability to worry about the problem for a while, eliminating possibilities and working your way to a solution is a highly effective character trait for a game designer.

What the Book Will Cover

This book is intended to take a practical approach, with examples and content which generalizes the best practices within game economy and monetization. Included are some guidelines to practices which can be observed in everyday professional game development workplaces.

I feel it is important to stress that this book was never written with the vision of becoming an encyclopedia of game economy design. It is written in digestible sections which have a natural order. There will be benefits to dipping in and out of certain sections, because these have standalone value, but in general it will be more prudent to start at the beginning and read the book from cover to cover.

The book starts with high-level theory and thought processes, then breaks this down into the minutiae, delving into lower-level details. In this sense, the approach mimics the fashion in which a designer would go about building a game economy.

We begin by introducing the building blocks of an economy, in the form of currencies and resources, and how these can be manipulated.

This will move into addressing key questions about player experience and feeling which will drive the economy design forward.

Detailed sections follow on from this, covering the design of the game economy components and metagame features, with techniques for scoping out their design using spreadsheet software and mathematics.

Monetization has many facets, so it is covered as a full section of its own. There is information on the various techniques which can be applied to different business models and how the focus of monetization changes depending on the strategies applied.

The development-related sections round off with information about work that is carried out post launch to maintain a game, with planning techniques and some examination of data analysis.

There is a chapter regarding the practical realities of working life in a professional development studio, and some hints on breaking into the industry.

The book concludes with case studies of some contemporary video games, analyzing them from an economy, metagame and monetization standpoint.

Reference

The Art of Game Design: A Book of Lenses, Jesse Schell, 2008

1

OUTLINING GAME ECONOMY DESIGN

What Is a Game Economy?

In real-world terms, an economy is the highly complex set of inter-related systems and activities concerning the production, consumption and exchange of resources, goods and services which fulfil the needs of individuals within a country or region. The word economy, however, can be used to describe inter-related systems and activities, across a vast range of smaller subdivisions including, for example companies or even a single family.

It is generally understood that game economy design concerns itself more with game design than traditional economics. While real-world economic theories and terminology are referenced and used to some extent, the game economy designer's role, along with other designers, is to create player engagement and, specifically, things for the players to do.

A game economy is a highly tailored, fabrication of a real-world economy, functioning around in-game resources, currencies and virtual goods, along with a system of engagements and activities for players. It is, in essence, a much simpler, controlled version of a real-world economy.

The aspects of a game which fall under the umbrella of game economy can be tricky to define, and different genres of games utilize game economy design in different ways. However, there are a number of components, practices and theoretical tools for the game economy designer to use, which will be discussed in the following sub-sections of this chapter.

What Does a Game Economy Designer Do?

Naturally the game economy designer's overarching task is to create the interweaving systems and flow of resources, goods and currencies

DOI: 10.1201/9781003386865-2

5

within the game: a game economy. The job itself is a subspecialty within the divisions of game design and can generally be thought of as concerning the design of the systems which relate to the long-term engagement of the player. This contrasts with the other design disciplines which are working on the minute-to-minute action-phase gameplay. Game economy design concerns itself with the areas of the game which include the control for distribution of content and rewards (broadly, a progression system), and the resources, goods and currencies which are used in tandem with these systems. By extension, the game economy designer is concerned with the monetization and microtransaction elements which have become more commonplace throughout games.

Essential to any role within the game design team is a high level of collaboration with colleagues. Game economy design is no different. There are certain aspects which absolutely lend themselves to two or more people sitting down in front of a computer screen and discussing the inner workings of a system. This will and should form a key part of the working day. The areas covered by you as a game economy designer will overlap one way or another with the work of a designer covering the many other systems in the game, including user interface and narrative. Beyond this, naturally you will collaborate with developers on the entire team. This is the spirit of game development, and it involves an intricate blend of technology, art, creativity and psychology, all mixed to produce fascinating end products to be enjoyed by millions.

Goals of a Game Economy

A fundamental question: why do we have the need for a game economy in the first place?

The concept of a game economy is utilized to varying degrees across the different genres of games, and it is true that not all genres require a standard game economy. From the early days of the games industry, many titles had little concept of such a game economy. However, as games developed over the years, new trends surfaced, and new types of gameplay experiences and engagement developed, and therefore so did the need for a game economy.

Game design as a discipline, and by extension the game designer as a role, is there to solve conceptual problems within the development cycle of a game, leading to an improved player experience. Ergo, game economy typically exists to solve a number of problems often concerned with the overall player journey and long-term engagement within a game.

A game economy facilitates direct player engagement. A game economy in this sense bleeds into the main action phase of a game (e.g. playing a mission in a shooter game, involving combat). As a game economy encompasses the systems related to player resources, goods and in-game currencies, these are used to give a degree of value and context to the goods that a player utilizes while playing.

A game economy provides long-term player experience. One of the key aspects to a game economy is to provide a motivation for long-term engagement within a game. The controlled distribution and usage of resources should keep players coming back over an extended period of time and allow the player to establish a routine of play on a regular basis.

A game economy acts as the access to and the control of distribution of content. Closely related to the motivation for long-term engagement is the need for control and by extension safety measures over the distribution of content. A game development team can only create a finite amount of content with the time and budget allowed for any project. If the pacing of the content is incorrect, players can potentially burn through this content far too quickly, ultimately causing the player to leave the game; i.e. if the player acquires the game's most valuable content with relative ease, what reason would they have to continue playing? The game economy and, in particular, the progression systems (see below) can act as metaphorical brakes on content distribution, ultimately preventing a potentially damaging content burn rate. Aside from preventing content burn, a game economy concerns itself with session control. In other words, the game must provide the player with just enough content: not too little, not too much during any given play session. The details of how long a play session should be will vary depending on the game itself, the genre, platform and target audience.

The concept of giving utility to players is achieved by this access to content. Think of an open world game, which opens up more as the player plays, giving access to more quests, side quests, collectables, skills and surprises along the way. Alternatively, a collectable card game gives the player an expanding pool of mechanics to use, thus creating strategic depth.

A game economy itself provides engagement and should generate fun. Often, the game economy is something which is generally "felt" by the player, as opposed to being noticed in the same moment to moment fashion as core gameplay mechanics. Naturally, creating a game economy interaction which features the same emotion, sensation and buzz of action gameplay would be an impossible task. However, the concept of an economy generating intrinsic fun for the player is an important design consideration. The narrative design and the nature of the project can also have an impact on this. For example, if a game features fly-by-night black market trading, this could provide some inherent intrigue to otherwise relatively mundane elements.

A game economy provides adaptability and growth. Many video games must be sustainable long after their initial launch, and postlaunch operations continuously update the game after its initial launch. The game economy must be built in such a way as to allow it to be expanded and modified. These updates can take many forms, such as new currencies and features which "plug into" the main game economy systems.

A game economy provides access to monetization, and depth of player spending. Monetization in the context of game economy design typically refers to the in-app/in-game purchases (microtransactions) that occur after the main game purchase or free download. These give the player access to premium (premium will be synonymous with "costing real money" throughout this book) features and content. With a strong game economy design, there will be a synergy between the regular economy and the premium (costing real money) content. One caveat is that the individual business model and game genre is a major determinant of how the game economy relates to monetization. Monetization will be covered in more detail within Chapter 4.

Key Components of the Game Economy

With the goals of a game economy in mind, what are the actual building blocks and theoretical components/elements which the economy designer has at his/her disposal?

Currencies

Currencies are a natural part of any economy, both virtual and real world. However, currencies do not necessarily need to exist in video games. There are many games which do not require currency and, by extension, do not have a typical game economy. This does not prevent these games from containing a progression system, and other resources for players to collect. For games which have a currency – that is, a medium of exchange – integrated into their design, the common convention is to design a soft currency, which is a currency that the player obtains from playing the game. The soft currency is used for purchases within the game that have a direct link to the gameplay and the player's engagement. For example, soft currencies are used as a charge for upgrading weapons and equipment used by the player. Many games take the design approach of having a single soft currency with a variety of uses spread across the game's features. This soft currency works in synergy with other more specific resources within the game, and free-to-play games typically often introduce other new soft currencies into their design, especially as these games adapt and evolve with updates post release.

Many games typically also introduce a hard currency. This is a currency that is acquired through real money microtransactions and can have a variety of applications. The most noteworthy use of a hard currency is for the purchase of purely cosmetic vanity items. These are often used for character customization such as items of clothing and accessories, but can also be special commands known as emotes, which players use to convey emotions or perform greetings to other players during a multiplayer game. Economy design does not preclude a hard currency from being dropped in small quantities through the gameplay. This is often used during the early stages of a game to teach the player the usage of hard currency and to help to drive potential further monetization.

Goods

Goods are items in the game that are tangible to the player. A good in this sense can be difficult to define. Broadly speaking, these are the major items that the players owns. Not all of these may relate directly to the game economy, although from a theoretical standpoint they do.

The items which are easily recognizable as goods tied to the game economy are weapons, armor pieces, cosmetic apparel and similar content tied to the in-game currencies. For example, a loot focused role-playing game will involve repeated cycles of buying and selling these items. Other items that can be viewed as goods are, for example, tools and gadgets which many action or stealth games often incorporate into their design. These items may simply be available to use, without significant links to the game economy, and are therefore of more concern to system designers. However, the game economy designer must be a stakeholder within their design, as the use of these items will have an impact on player performance and can have a knock-on effect on other aspects of the game economy, for example, the rate at which players progress and acquire currencies and resources.

Resources

Resources can also be difficult to define, as there is often an overlap between goods and currencies, but there are typically differences to note. Resources are often collected for a specific purpose and combined or utilized within one or more of the game's systems. They are typically precursor items used in the production of other items and are collected in abundance throughout a game environment or via core gameplay.

A common type of resource which many will encounter includes crafting materials found in modern action role-playing games. For example, the player must collect the resource called "metal fragments", which can be taken to a blacksmith non-player character, who will use these metal fragments to craft a new sword for the player. These types of resources are usually distributed in abundance and can help to provide a method for designers of large scale – particularly open world – titles to extensively populate the game environment with numerous amounts of minor rewards.

Although not generally thought of as a resource, experience points which are awarded through gameplay would be broadly classified as a resource for the player. These may not be used in the direct sense, but they contribute to other systems, unlocks and rewards. They would differ from a currency, as they cannot be spent by the player. There is a similarity here with professional sports leagues, where teams accumulate points from winning matches.

A word of caution regarding terminology. The term "resource" will commonly be used as an over-arching term for all elements of a game economy, from currencies to content. Keep context in mind while researching.

Sources

A source can also be called a faucet, or a tap in British English. A source is defined as a means within the game by which players receive in-game currency, resources or goods. In the context of a virtual game economy, the currency, resource or good is created from nothing and injected into the economy. With a source created, the game economy designer has the task of adjusting how much currency (or resources/goods) this source provides to the player.

Typically, the most prominent source within a game economy is that which generates in-game soft currency. Sources for soft currency are used as a method for providing the main reward for the player's engagement with the core gameplay. As the currency is generated from everyday engagement by the player, this can often generate a large amount of currency simply by existing, in turn creating the main balancing task for the designer. An example would be an amount of soft currency which the player receives for completing a level in a mobile puzzle game.

The source for resources is another type which you will encounter within a game economy. Designers often use more bespoke means to generate resources for players, entirely dependent on the type of game and the business model, to solve problems in the design or guide the player to playing the game in a specific method or pattern.

Consider a system where the player must upgrade weapons, and after reaching the maximum level, the player can begin levelling up the weapon again from zero, but this time with new powered-up features on the weapon permanently available. In order to reset the weapon, the player must use a rare resource only acquired from completing specific weekly missions within the game. The use of these therefore guides the player into a weekly engagement with the game, controlling the means by which the player can upgrade weapons.

Sources for goods can be more difficult to define and are not to be confused with traders (see section below). Sources for goods, like resources, are often used to solve specific design problems, but can be a main part of the game's core engagement. For example, many role-playing games function around the collection of loot; items dropped by enemies. An example would be a sword dropped by a monster after the player kills it, within a fantasy role-playing game. Sources for goods can also provide the player with certain rewards for regular engagement with the game, to aid retention. An example would be a consumable health potion which is given to the player for returning to the game a specific number of times within a set period (though in practice, currency is used more predominantly in this instance).

Sinks

A sink (sometimes called a drain) is a way or object/element within the game which removes currency, resources or goods from the economy. A sink destroys the currency, resource or good, removing it permanently. Sinks are used to combat currency inflation and work in conjunction with sources. It is also the task of the designer to balance the sinks to remove sufficient currency, resources or goods relative to the rate at which the sources are generating.

A sink for currency can initially seem obvious to design but can quickly become tricky to add to a game while keeping a sense of credibility within the experience and the established narrative of the game. Definitions become more obscure with currency sinks relative to the type of game. Take the example of purchasing a store item. Within the context of a single player game without player-to-player trading, this can act as a currency sink, with the currency being taken out of the economy. We should note that this currency is being replaced by a good. In essence, this behaves more like a *converter* (see below). Naturally, the player must get something in return for spending their hard-earned currency, so finding intricate ways of removing the currency while giving something in return which is continually needed and desired, something moreover that can be given repeatedly over the player's lifetime with the game, is a key design challenge. Within a game which involves player trading, buying items from other players would not act as a sink at all, as the *trader* (see below) would exchange the currency and the good between the two parties. Given the fact that soft currency is readily printed by playing a game, it naturally tends to be in abundance, with designers left straining to find ways to remove it. A few examples of currency sinks would be: an amount of soft currency charged for upgrading a piece of equipment, or an amount of currency charged to begin a new match, which may be used for certain game modes in multiplayer titles.

The concept of sinks for resources may be used for specific cases within the game. Resources tend to have controlled distribution relative to the game and are given very specific uses, so their need for blatant sinks is not the same as for currencies. Resources function effectively with *converters* (see below), for example where they can be transformed into goods. This would effectively be a sink for the resource and a source for the good.

Sinks for goods can take different forms, and game designers often come up with quite innovative ways to remove items from a player, again specific to the genre and business model of the game. Role-playing games often allow players to sell unwanted items to non-player character vendors, in return for small amounts of currency or resources. While this is theoretically a trade, the good is being destroyed by the vendor, and the amount of currency given back is typically a fraction of the amount that the good was purchased with. In certain cases, games may feature items or weapons which are permanently lost, for example if the player character is killed during a mission.

Converters

Converters are mechanics which transform one type of good, currency or resource into another within the game. A useful way of thinking about the converter is that it is acting as a source and sink simultaneously, producing one element in return for instantly destroying another. While this can be applied in many ways within games, the most obvious use of the converter lies within the design of crafting systems, or the harvesting of resources or similar mechanics within strategy, or construction and city building simulation games. For example, players will collect certain raw resources deposited from the game environment and will use these in conjunction with a non-player character (e.g. a blacksmith) to create a new tool or weapon.

The use of converters can be applied across many genres of games and can be used as part of puzzle solving within games, or indeed any system whereby players collect multiple components and then combine these into a single whole item. The behavior of the converter should not be described as a variation of a sink. Although the number of elements can be reduced, the converter does not totally destroy anything without replacing it with something else. It is a theoretical tool at the disposal of the game economy designer, to be utilized in various situations.

Traders

Traders are mechanics which exchange goods, resources or currencies between different entities within the game. As a definition this can seem overly technical, but in practice the trader is a theoretical way of describing the behavior of, for example, a player purchasing a weapon from another player, for an amount of in-game money. The trader mechanic transfers in-game money from the account of Player A to the account of Player B and transfers the weapon from the account of Player B to the account of Player A. This is where we can observe the nuances of traders and the overlap between traders and sinks. If the player buys a new item from a non-player vendor character, this is not trader functionality. From the player's perspective it appears to be the same, i.e. they give away one element and receive a different one in return. But in this instance, the player is interacting with the game which destroys the in-game currency and creates an item out of nothing to give to the player. A trader as a theoretical object must not destroy or create anything, it simply exchanges different existing elements between entities in the game. Even within a game which involves player to player trading, from the perspective of one player, the trader appears to act like a converter on the surface, but in terms of the overall economic balance, and crucially for the designer, the two are different.

Game Genre and Business Models

For those of us who have had a strong passion for video games from a young age, the concept of genre is something from which we derive our main emotional connection to the games we enjoy. As the years go by and we purchase new devices, and their associated titles, we connect to specific types of games and find new favorites, and obsessions.

Over the ever-changing landscape of the games industry, the factors constituting the different game genres have also changed. There is still a lot of ambiguity, with many games breaking trends, and fusing defining elements from different genres.

What defines a game's genre? Genre is the French word for type, and the term is often heard in the context of films. However, what characterizes the video game medium is that genre mainly refers to the type of gameplay involved, as opposed to the type of story being told. Some of the main video game genres with which I have always associated personally are the following:

- First-person shooter
- Action adventure
- Sports
- Racing
- Puzzle
- Strategy

There are a plethora of sub-genres within each of these, and the list could extend for many pages.

How are these different genres relevant to the game economy? Naturally, some genres lend themselves to a typical game economy far more than others, but there is a large gray area in between the extremes which includes varying aspects and elements of a game economy. A strategy game such as *Clash of Clans* features a prominent game economy and metagame, while a story-driven adventure or interactive drama title may feature no game economy in the immediate sense. However, there may be progression systems built into a story-driven game, even if they are not prominent and player facing, so the generic principles and theory within this book should be able to be readily applied whenever the needs arise.

At this point, it becomes necessary to address the two major business models that dominate the games industry: *Free-to-Play* and *Premium*.

Free-to-Play

A game which follows the free-to-play business model is available for players to play without any upfront real money cost and is the dominant business model for mobile games. Monetization is built into the game via the use of non-compulsory microtransactions, which the player can carry out from within the game. The microtransactions provide the user with some benefit(s), closely related to the game's design, such as content, or some other more optimal experience for the player to enjoy.

Monetization should be built into the game from the ground up and be considered during development as part of the process of building the game's economy. Tagging on a monetization strategy at the end of a project will inevitably lead to a more mediocre result.

A pattern of effective design for free-to-play games tends to involve a single core method of play, which takes place in consistently measurable play sessions, and from here the player builds an expression around this core experience, with engagement, retention and ultimately monetization features wrapped around this. A good example of this would be the game *Rocket League*, which shifted business models to free-to-play, from originally being a premium title. The game centers around multiplayer matches, with other features such as tournaments, customization and live events all complementing this single user experience (Figure 1.1).

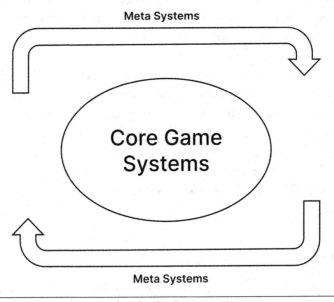

Figure 1.1 Typical gameplay loop for a free-to-play game.

Premium Product

Premium games are games in which the player must pay an upfront cost. Many of the most popular franchises on PC and console are premium products.

As a premium experience demands that a player part with real money before beginning to play, there is more leeway for the game to be a self-contained journey, which combines different challenges, rhythms of engagement, types of gameplay and experiences (Figure 1.2).

A single player, open world, story-driven game could be considered an archetype for this, with a narrative that changes, progresses and adapts to context, combined with a mixture of combat and problem-solving gameplay, and many other surprises along the way.

There are exceptions to this, with some sports and racing games being genres which could conveniently lend themselves to the free-to-play type of engagement. It is worth bearing in mind that these games are often high budget, yearly iterating franchises, with licenses from sports associations, and often in themselves contain expansive career and season modes, requiring a large time investment from the player.

Paymium is a term that can be used to refer to the practice of a premium game also including the opportunity for further in-game microtransactions.

I feel the need to make a small qualification in relation to the detailed chapters which form the remainder of this book. It is certainly true that a great deal of game economy and monetization design has its heart in the free-to-play model, and this should be taken into consideration. However, bearing in mind the readership for this book,

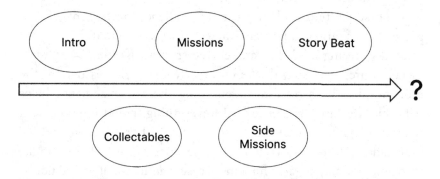

Figure 1.2 Player engagement diagram for a typical premium product.

and the changing nature of the games industry, I have attempted to generalize the concept of game economy to systems which can be applied to solve meta design-related problems within different games. These potential solutions will be largely independent of the business model the project is using, but will also allow for the perception that some genres lend themselves to game economy more than others. Often, there is overlap between free-to-play and premium design, and the methodologies can be readily applied across different projects. By extension, game design can be boiled down to a series of problems to solve whatever interconnected systems are present. Therefore, it is very relevant as an economy designer to think of and apply the theory to whichever project-specific problems present themselves, and to be able to, for example, use and reapply free-to-play best practices in a premium game where relevant and whenever the needs arise.

Now we will begin the deep dive, by first looking at the high-level driving force behind the game economy, in "player motivation".

Player Motivation

As a prelude to going into the specifics of building the game economy, it is important to start asking the most high-level questions about the overall design of the game, which is, in essence, part of the game's overall direction. This is something which must happen before pre-production fully starts, and is usually handled within a small team, including the game director who sets the creative vision for the project. To get to the bottom of player motivation, and with the business model being already decided, there are a series of questions which will help set the scene for the metagame.

The first question is who is the target audience for the game? Every game needs a target audience. Different titles appeal to different people, with varying life habits and character traits. Keeping the game's meta features in line with the overall creative vision is part of the economy designer's role, and identifying the target audience helps with this. The target audience guides everything about the game, from the type of content and features to the pacing of progression, and the multitude of decisions that will be made along the way. For example, if you are building a game for a more casual audience, it would not be sensible to spend a lot of development resources building an incredibly deep series of meta systems which are not going to be discovered by the majority of players. Likewise, an economy which is too simplistic would not appeal to the audience of a more hardcore game.

The second question is what are the main emotions that the game's design wants to generate in players? You need to identify how you would like your players to feel while playing the game, and how these feelings connect with each other. These involve everything from the waves of emotion that occur during a single round of gameplay, and during a single play session, all the way through to the overarching emotions over the player's lifetime with the game. Is there anything in particular you are looking to ignite in players? There are many different emotions that are intrinsic to video games, and the design of the metagame and economy can play on these. Satisfaction, happiness and surprise can be powerful positive emotions to generate in players. However, you must also look to conjure up more negative emotions such as frustration and disappointment along the way. A game requires this to complement the positive times. Pride and envy, which are themselves extremely powerful feelings, can also be exploited.

With insights gained from the first two questions, the third question is: what are players going to be doing within the game? This will typically adhere closely to the genre of the game. Take a step back into the persona of the player and ask the question, what am I doing in a game? Naturally, the first answer that comes to mind is trivial. In a racing game you are racing vehicles, probably cars in some form. But really, there are sub-genres within this, with their own experiences that cater to different players. There is often one over-arching goal, but there are many different segments of player experience to take into consideration. For example, a game could involve engaging in quick races, to build up a collection of vehicles, with upgrades helping with this collection process. The game could have a story mode, various multiplayer modes and ranked leagues. What are the predominant elements to consider, and how do they come together into a coherent whole?

Developing an Economy

The natural follow-on from the previous questions is to take the answers and put them into more of a context within a system of components which help to build up a working game economy. With the

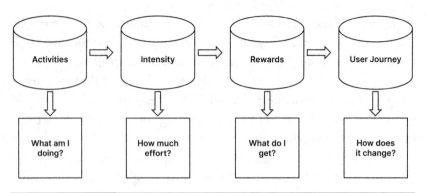

Figure 1.3 Diagram showing the highest level of theoretical game economy components.

knowledge of the components of the economy, we can now think about the overall experience of the game, and what the player is doing in terms of the gameplay. This can be seen as a hypothetical directional thought process to ignite the game economy.

We can address the highest-level theory of the economy by thinking through and answering questions related to the following topics: Activities, Intensity, Rewards and User Journey (Figure 1.3).

Activities

What are the core activities that happen within the game, through the different types of gameplay in relation to the game economy? Ultimately you are addressing the question of what the things are that players are doing. This could be the main story battles that onboard new players and keep them engaged for multiple subsequent play sessions. Other examples could involve quick battles, daily challenges or end-game boss raids.

Intensity

The intensity takes the activities and contextualizes them in terms of how much time and effort they require from the player. This will then be used to define what type of rewards they tie into. For example, an end-game boss raid would require far more valuable, rare rewards compared to a simple daily logon reward, which would require a small amount of the game's main (and easy-to-acquire) soft currency. This is an important step. It may seem like common sense, but it is important during the course of development to identify and keep a measure of the type or quantity of rewards that are given through different gameplay modes or features, and how these may potentially change. During the cold reality of game development, it is quite common to be pushed into re-using certain rewards. Economy designers can find themselves not differentiating sufficiently between easy-to-acquire and extremely grind-focused rewards, which in turn has a detrimental effect on the player's overall engagement.

Rewards

This step requires the designer to define the currencies which will drive the economy. In addition to this, the resources can be considered. In reality, the line between currencies and resources can become blurry. The goods which serve as rewards must also be defined, and in general how these all tie together. This stage involves asking the question "why does the player care about investing in this economy?"

User Journey

At this stage you will be considering the overall user journey of the player. This ties heavily into the overall progression system (regardless of how prominent and/or complex the progression system is). It is this section that will serve as the initial spark for the more complex design of the user journey. At this point you must reflect on how things will change over time from a high-level standpoint.

There is an early onboarding phase, which can be more contrived and designer controlled. The player investment is small at this point and should therefore require minimal effort. There will be a mid-level phase where players are in the system, with less predictability around the player's experience. Last, although not relevant to all players, an end-game phase for the most experienced and skilled individuals must be considered.

We must ask ourselves, what do we do to keep players going forward? What activities are unlocking, and what types of rewards and currencies are focused on during certain points within the user journey. For example, how are these rewards distributed at the end game compared to the mid-game phases?

At this stage, it will be prudent to roughly map out the stages of the user journey on paper, which will serve as the basis for planning the deeper, detailed design to follow.

Reference

Virtual Economies: Design and Analysis, Vili Lehdonvirta and Edward Castronova, 2014

2
GAME ECONOMY AND THE METAGAME

With the theory and the components of a game economy defined in the previous chapter, this chapter will take these components and cover the details of how they are used in building a game economy. Game economy design (and indeed any branch of game design) involves taking a set of theoretical tools and using them in different ways to solve problems and create engaging experiences.

Naturally the minutiae of building a game economy are tied to the specific project which one is building and the unique problems and goals this presents during the course of development. However, within the industry, there is a recognized and effective angle of approach to building games. This can be summarized in the sense that one must first look at the big picture, or the entire experience, prototype core mechanics as quickly as possible, test and then iterate. This contrasts with the idea of creating and refining a section of a game early on, before adding new sections, which is not a particularly healthy or helpful approach and will tend to create mediocre results.

While this can be difficult to accurately define on paper, it can be illustrated with examples. Consider the game of Chess. This game creates tremendous depth from a relatively simple set of rules involving the different movement and attack properties of the various playing pieces. The artistic appearance of the playing pieces with their war theme is purely a skin over the gameplay. If you were to design the game functionally today, you would prototype it out on paper with placeholder pieces, make sure all the mechanics were working and only then would you consider the visual appearance of the pieces. You would not begin by intricately carving out the King and Queen playing pieces and then try to add others to the board and strain to fit the gameplay around them.

DOI: 10.1201/9781003386865-3

A past project on which I worked involved creating a puzzle game inspired heavily by the Rubik's Cube. As part of the creation process, our team purchased a Rubik's Cube, along with some stickers and glue, and pieced together a physical prototype before going anywhere near a computer. Despite being well over a decade ago, this was still a seminal design moment for me.

The design of a game economy is no different and still adheres to this key principle. The overall experience must be visualized as a collective whole and then refined. In practice this becomes complicated, as there will be many different features that feed into the economy, and, of course, systems change and adapt during the development timeline of a project. Also, this overall approach applies to the game as a whole, but with complex modern games with many modes, features and mechanics, this process can be applied on multiple granular levels.

It is important to build projects with this prototyping approach in mind and not stray from it as development progresses. The following sections consider taking a step back and visualizing the entire game economy.

The Core Loop

Almost any contemporary video game can be thought of as a repeated cycle (loop) of action or intense engagement, broken up by times of respite in between. This can take different forms. For example, a linear action-adventure game will involve periods of combat, interspersed with slower paced puzzles and problem solving, or cutscenes. For different genres, this same high-level concept takes different forms. For a title such as *Rocket League*, the intense engagement, which we can call the action phase, occurs with the player taking part in matches. Outside of these matches, the player is essentially resting within the front-end menus of the game. These contain information which relates to the experience, such as summaries of the cosmetics a player owns, lists of daily or weekly challenges to take part in, seasonal event invitations and more. Essentially, the player experiences the game in a continuous loop of engagement, moving between action and resting, shown in Figure 2.1.

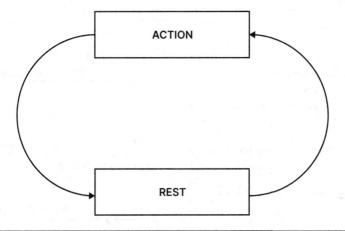

Figure 2.1 Diagram showing a player engagement loop of action and resting.

The game economy components exist within this structure, and from these interesting loops of gameplay, the game economy must be felt by the player, in the developing rapport that they will experience when repeating this action-rest loop many times. The designer's intention is to develop this into a habit.

With this basic theory in mind, the first port of call is to take a step back and visualize the big picture of the game economy you are trying to create. First, consider your resources and the goods that are present in the game, then map this out into a core loop flow diagram, which considers the sinks and sources for these resources, along with the purpose of the different aspects of the game. This can be thought of as a more detailed, zoomed-in version of Figure 2.1.

The most effective way to illustrate the creation of a core loop is to take an example of a hypothetical game, with a description of the player experience, and then visualize the core loop in Figure 2.2.

The game, which will be generally referred to as Project X for the remainder of this book, is a mobile free-to-play, first-person shooting game, where the player competes in player-versus-player matches. The game is about progressing and unlocking weapons, which must be upgraded. The game features two main currencies:

1. *Cash*, which is the soft currency obtained from playing matches.
2. *Gold*, which is the hard currency obtained from real money microtransactions.

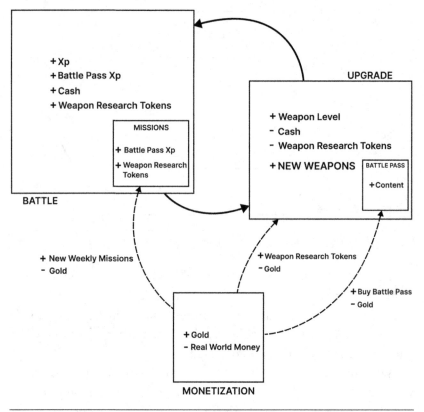

Figure 2.2 Diagram showing detailed core loop of a hypothetical example game.

From playing matches, the player also obtains:

- *Experience points* which are used to level up the player's account. This forms the main progression system within the game and governs the unlocking of new weapons.
- *Weapon Research Tokens* which are used in conjunction with in-game *Cash* to upgrade weapons. Applying Weapon Research Tokens to a weapon, in turn, applies upgrade points to that weapon, causing it to level up. Each weapon level unlocks new modifications for that weapon. There are different types of tokens available, which are specific to certain types of weapons, such as Assault Rifle Tokens and Shotguns Tokens. There are small, medium and large tokens for each, applying increasingly more upgrade points, respectively.

The game also features a Battle Pass which gives the player cosmetic items and requires specific *Battle Pass Experience Points* to progress, which are awarded through completing weekly missions.

For this game, we have two distinct phases involving action and resting, called Battle and Upgrade, respectively. There is also a separate section called Monetization which essentially complements the core loop, so is distinct. Not all core loop visualizations require the designer to address monetization, but I personally find it helpful to keep things tied together for when the design is expanded upon further down the line.

The player plays matches (within the Battle section) and from these will earn experience points along with a small quantity of Battle Pass Experience Points. The player will also earn Cash from the matches and a random drop of a number of Weapon Research Tokens.

As a subset of the main gameplay, the player will engage with daily and weekly missions which will give out Battle Pass Experience Points in larger quantities than the small amount given for the main matches. As a Battle Pass runs over the course of a number of weeks, the weekly mission rewards are designed to tie into this, with predefined amounts of Battle Pass Experience Points. There will also be Weapon Research Tokens assigned as rewards to some of the weekly missions.

When we get to the upgrade phase, the player is spending (or consuming) their earned Cash and Weapon Research Tokens to increase the level of a weapon. Alongside this, the player unlocks new weapons as a result of the main experience points acquired.

As a subset of the upgrade phase, we come back to the Battle Pass feature, where the player increases their Battle Pass level as a result of acquiring Battle Pass Experience Points. (See Chapter 4 for more information about Battle Passes.)

The final aspect to consider is the Monetization component. The player can spend real-world money to acquire the game's hard currency called Gold. The Gold can be used in several ways that connect to the core game loop as shown. First, Gold is used to buy the Battle Pass and allow the player to gain access to more desirable cosmetic content as they increase their Battle Pass level. To complement this, the player can spend Gold to gain access to more weekly missions than they otherwise would without spending

Gold. Therefore, after spending Gold the player is still required to engage in gameplay. We are using real money payment as a means of giving better rewards more quickly, without removing the need to actually play the game. Finally, the player can also use Gold to purchase an offering of Weapon Research Tokens (potentially by way of gacha mechanics), allowing the player to expedite their weapon progression.

For this high-level gameplay loop, it is not necessary to put too much detail into the specific behavior of resources within this high-level diagram. Do not muddy the water. Specific details such as the base experience points the player gains from entering matches, the micro experience point rewards for enemy kills, along with multipliers for winning the matches compared to losing, are something that is a more complex part of the metagame design and can be detailed within part of the game's design documentation. It is not necessary information for this high-level core loop. In essence, we simply need to establish that experience points are given directly from playing matches at this stage.

It is important for a core loop to remain, but often this will expand to outer loops concerning certain over-arching meta related features. This can be handled on a case-by-case basis and can come into play as part of the postlaunch live operations of a game.

There is no standard method for visualizing a core loop, and a common sense approach is often best, based on the overall engagement loop that you are trying to design. It is up to you as the designer to visualize it in the manner that suits yourself and, importantly, the other team members working on the project.

For reference to core game loops, I would recommend reading analyses of existing games, in particular on websites such as *Deconstructor of Fun*. A solid critical evaluation of a game should begin by looking into the core resources flow, and from there breaking down the components into more detail, eventually leading into deductions about the performance and long-term experience for the player. While analyzing an existing game can be quite different to building a new system yourself, it still provides a lot of learning. There will be problems that other games solve, which you can apply to your own game. Knowing how, why and when to do this simply takes practice and experience.

Metagame Components and Design

The term "meta" in video games has a number of different meanings. First, in the competitive gaming scene, or eSports communities, meta refers to finding dominant strategies within games, i.e. using combinations of items, characters or weapons in-game which are more effective than others. The meta in this sense are ways of playing that emerge from the core mechanics that designers have put in place, and these continuously change with updates causing certain strategies or items to become more or less effective. This definition of meta tends to be associated with end users, rather than developers, and is not the definition utilized by this book.

Metagame, which this entire book is designed to explore, refers to the set of systems and mechanics which surround the main core gameplay. These systems involve their own loops of engagement which wrap around the core gameplay and drive the long-term player experience. Game economy intertwines itself with the metagame in every way. This means that trying to scientifically define the differences between the metagame and the game economy can be challenging. Sometimes these two terms can almost be used interchangeably, as they refer to the same systems. One way of thinking about it is that the metagame is composed of a series of systems that are outside the core action phase gameplay, whereas the game economy is a theoretical concept which is felt and experienced by players across many parts of the game. The game economy is born from the metagame components. Despite this, your goal as the designer is to provide an experience that players will enjoy and stay with, so the nuances of definitions and terminology can be flexible.

Primarily, the metagame is derived from the core loop section described earlier within this chapter. Visualizing the core loop involves taking a step back, and considering the overall player experience which surrounds the core gameplay, including the flows of resources and goods. From here we move into the specifics of each feature and analyze how they work, how they contribute to the player experience and economy, how they interweave and cause certain effects and ultimately drive desired player behavior.

This design process is not only a big topic, but it is very game specific. To save this chapter from becoming a fully-fledged design for a game, the next section will instead cover specific elements which comprise the metagame and game economy, detailing each element and how it can be used. You can think of this as the designer's toolbox or a series of best practices for creating the metagame, with an overall game economy taking shape as a result.

Progression System Design

A progression system is an important part of the metagame and is used by the economy designer for different purposes. Progression systems take many forms depending on the design goals and the type of game being developed.

To take an example of progression systems from the world beyond video games, let's consider the analogy of a person who decides to take up a new hobby, such as tennis. What journey would this person expect to take from beginning tennis, to moving toward advanced levels? You would expect there to be some type of initial hook which gets them interested; a type of trial which may be a summer taster session, a beginner's course, or they may simply just go to their first class. Whatever the case, they will start in a beginner's group and be taught the fundamental skills required for tennis. They will remain in the beginner's group, practicing these base skills until they improve enough to move to a slightly more skilled group, where they will be challenged and driven to improve on the fundamentals. This is the point where they may feel the frustration of having to consider many components of the learning experience simultaneously, and the need to persist until muscle memory takes over and general skills come more naturally. After this they would enter an intermediate group, where they would start to build more advanced techniques and strategies. Without the foundations, the style of training in the intermediate group would be counter-productive, so progression is required. At this level, the training would take on a more personal character, where the individual's own strengths and weaknesses are taken into account, and can be improved and built upon. At this point a greater time commitment is required, and there are significant challenges. Eventually the player would move into more advanced groups and expect to be extremely committed. Tennis would become a major part of their life. Challenges would increase, and the time investment and competitive nature of the sport would become more apparent. With the player having solid foundations and advanced skills, these would constantly be worked on, but a lot of fine tuning would also take place. After hitting this advanced level, there will be multiple tiers of elite ability, all the way from a lower-level full time professional to the superstars that we all know. This outline could serve as a breakdown of the progression system of tennis or, in fact, any new sport, but this real-world experience of a progression system could also be applied to progression system design within the world of video games.

Earlier video games featured a natural progression to teach players the rudiments of the game and then keep them challenged and interested. This is akin to the difficulty curve within platform games such as *Super Mario Bros* or *Sonic the Hedgehog*. The early levels teach the basic skills and condition the player for what will come later, for example, teaching the player to jump over a gap, without necessarily failing as a result of missing the jump. The difficulty increases over subsequent levels by way of introducing increasingly more complex maneuvers and new gameplay elements such as different dangers, traps and enemies. The experience is clearly divided into separate levels and worlds and augmented with several boss battles notably increasing in difficulty. This separation provides the player with milestones within their feeling of achievement over the course of the game. They have an oscillating cycle of intensity with the challenges they face, followed by the respite after completing these challenges. Overall, and with good game design, the challenges presented match the player's skill level sufficiently to keep them interested but not out of their depth. If the game does not increase the difficulty of the challenges it presents, the player will quickly lose interest. If the challenges increase in difficulty too steeply, this will cause too much frustration and again, the player will lose interest.

This fundamental task of planning out a user's engagement with an interest in the game is what makes progression system design what it is today, but the ways in which this is achieved has seen many iterations, innovations, expansions and complications.

This brings us to the wider usage of progression systems. The design of modern progression systems is intricate and typically involves some form of system by which players level up, measured numerically by successive levels. This often becomes an interconnected web of features which expand, gaining in power or accessibility as the player puts more hours into the game. Progression systems are used to teach the player and allow them to establish a habit of playing the game. They are used to control access to game elements and allow the player to try to learn new strategies as their competency and skills level increase. They are also used to control content distribution. From the designer's standpoint, they allow us to plan and manipulate the experience for players and can link to analytics, allowing us in-depth analysis of different player groups. This in turn allows us to discover which parts of the design work and which do not.

Progression Systems and the User Journey

From a game directional standpoint, the planning of a progression system (and its associated economy aspects) begins with the overall user journey. This involves planning out the early stages where a new player is introduced to the game's systems (known as the onboarding stages), the middle stages of the player life cycle with the game, through to the later stages and the features which will cater to the most dedicated of players.

One caveat applying to the following sections (and indeed all metagame and economy design) is that I attempt to generalize the overall user journey for players irrespective of the genre of game being developed and even across the different business models within the games industry. For free-to-play games, as the player has not invested anything into the game in order to start and continue playing, you may see a more marked separation between the different phases of the progression system and more pronounced retention and engagement systems. For a premium product, the use of a progression system can be more subtle and more forgiving. It may even try to experiment more. The player has paid an upfront fee for the game and therefore has already invested and is naturally inclined to be more retained. This does not, however, preclude the game designer from having to focus on the interest level of the player, especially considering the amount of competition with games on the market. Chapter 4 covering monetization focuses on the more specific details of the different business models.

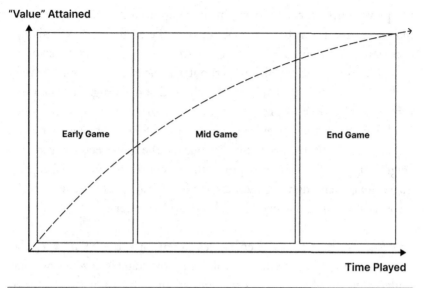

"Value" Attained

Early Game

Mid Game

End Game

Time Played

Figure 2.3   Graph showing the value players attain versus time played, with phases highlighted.

Figure 2.3 shows a generic progression curve within a game, with the X-axis representing the time since the player installed the game and the Y-axis representing the general amount of value or power that the player gains by playing the game. This can be thought of as a hypothetical value when planning out the overall user journey, considering various parts of the game. A levelling-up system and the control of reward distribution will use linked mathematical modeling and likely will attempt to mirror this type of curve. This shape of graph summarizes one key pillar of progression systems. That is, in the early phases they provide rapid progress, which levels off the more time that is spent within the game, while toward the endgame, there is little extra value or power added. It is not generally possible to add vast amounts of power on top of already high power. This is the point where players need different and varied types of engagement with game features.

Onboarding and Early Phase   A player begins their gameplay experience with an onboarding phase. At this point, the player has no knowledge of the game's systems. From a fresh install, the game will typically hook the player with some type of intense action sequence which introduces the core gameplay. This establishes the core mechanic that the player will expect to learn, improve upon and repeat while playing the game. From here, the player is in the early stages and should experience a certain rapid progress. They should expect to level up and gain some early abilities without the need for excessive effort, and they must feel that they have achieved something. This phase is typically composed of pre-defined, linear gameplay, such as the story mode, in which the player will begin to get a feel for the regular habit of playing, via daily or weekly challenges. The game economy at this stage is typically built in a pre-defined, contrived way, to keep all players experiencing roughly the same quantities of currencies, goods, resources, items and everything else the game offers.

Mid Phase   The mid phase continues to reinforce the habit of regular engagement with the game. The player at this stage is developing their understanding of the game's systems, identifying what they want to get out of the game and developing personal preferences and strategies. The player may engage with new modes and be using the game's social features, such as guilds. Economy-wise, the player will have obtained sufficient amounts of different items, goods and resources which feed into the game's systems and will be planning out spending for themselves. They are in the system and have the chance to find strategies within the economy.

End-Game Phase   At the end-game phase, players are not going to be getting a vast amount of new content. They have been experiencing the main game for a significant amount of time. It is now that it is desirable for players to be moved onto new experiences that give a broader way of engaging. Depending on the game in question, players could move from player-versus-environment modes into player-versus-player modes, where leaderboards come into play. There may be difficult dungeon raids within a role playing game. Rules can be updated and the concept of seasons utilized with resetting of certain progression elements (monthly or quarterly) and rotating rewards. There are many techniques to keep end-game players within the game, but it is vital that these players should get something out of the game that early game players do not. There is little reason for someone to dedicate significantly more of their free time to a game, to progress to the end and not be given some type of unique reward. Coming back to the real-world sport analogy of tennis, an amateur level player who enjoys engaging with the game on a casual basis will never get the same rewards as a world tour professional whose rewards may involve many desirable factors, including prize money. Another interesting point to bear in mind regarding the endgame of the user journey is how this applies across many games, even without a notable game economy. Later entries in the action-adventure series Uncharted are narrative driven single player games, but there are multiplayer components, and this keeps players engaged long after they have completed the main story.

Progression Systems as Content Control

Another use of progression systems is to control the distribution of content to players. This acts as the brake on the economy, allowing the designer to speed up and slow down the player's progress and place a hard block on the player acquiring too much too soon.

The main method for controlling the distribution of content within the game will be through an account level, an overarching series of levels through which the player will progress by playing the game. This concept of an account level can be used to lock cosmetic content behind individual levels, lock access to parts of a game environment and lock new gameplay features and potentially new game modes.

These levels not only control what the player has access to, but they allow for the designers to measure which stage different players have reached in their life cycle, which in turn has many benefits in terms of telemetry and data analysis (for live content design and development).

Vertical Progression

Vertical progression is a type of progression which refers to the direct increase in the power of gameplay elements. There is a clear differentiation of power, where some items, such as weapons, become more powerful than others. This system could be tied to the upgrading of equipment, whereby carrying out upgrades directly increases the power of the item. This type of progression can be observed within single player games, where the player discovers more powerful weapons as they progress through the story. These would be necessary to defeat the stronger enemies that appear toward the game's climax. Vertical progression is used within some player-versus-player games, such as collectible card games, where players upgrade the power of individual cards as part of the progression system.

Horizontal Progression

Horizontal progression refers to progression where the player gains a wider variety of content, which gives more varied and deep ways to play. No item is strictly better or worse than another, but there is more variety which yields more strategic depth. This type of progression can be observed in games which are likely to be purely skill-based, player-versus-player focused and are deliberately trying to adhere to the design pillar of not allowing clear-cut differentiation in power between gameplay elements. This can be observed in the weapon progression seen within the multiplayer components of *Call of Duty: Modern Warfare* (2019) whereby playing with a weapon generates experience points for that weapon, causing it to level up, while on successive levels a new modification for that weapon is unlocked. These modifications can take the form of new sights, foregrips, barrels, etc. These affect the weapon statistics in positive and negative ways, and the combination of different modifications applied to the weapon creates configurations which exhibit various properties. Although the challenge for the designer is not to create some modifications which are simply stronger than others, if created well, great depth of play can be produced, without mistakenly crafting accidental vertical progression.

Rarity Systems

The concept of rarity associated with specific items within video games has a unique meaning. A rarity is a classification of the item, typically shown by color coding the appearance of the item icons within the in-game store or inventory. There are usually around five rarities of items within each game, although there can be a few more or less. The conventions within contemporary games have come to name the rarities: Common, Uncommon, Rare, Epic and Legendary. The meaning of the different rarities depends on the design of the game. The higher rarity items are generally more powerful, or have additional properties that the lower rarities do not. Within a role-playing game focusing on the collection of swathes of items (and duplicates of items), the lower rarity content would drop in vast quantities, with higher rarities becoming heavily sought after. This raises the question of why do games use these rarity classifications? There are a number of reasons. Rarity can give players an instant recognition of the average quality levels of the many items available, relative to each other; something which is useful when a catalogue of content has many hundreds of items. In this sense, the rarity can give the players an indication of whether a particular weapon will be effective against certain enemies, at different levels. Rarity can enhance the sense of scarcity of certain items and create a strong emotional attachment in players for the Epic and Legendary items available. I have worked on a system where, after filling up the inventory with Common, Uncommon and Rare items through normal story missions, the special end-game dungeon raids would typically be the main way to earn Epic items, but had a chance of dropping a Legendary item. This became a major driver for players to grind at these dungeon raids in the hopes of landing these special legendary weapons.

For the economy designer, rarity can be a relatively cheap way to artificially expand the catalogue of content and integrate this into the progression system. As an example, weapons within a game can use the same 3D model, but can be duplicated five times, given different statistical values, and shown within the inventory screens with different colored icons for each rarity. This is far less work both in terms of time and creativity than modeling five unique weapons.

Alternatively, rarity can also be used to simply signify the level of "coolness" of an item. This is effectively used for items that are purely cosmetic in nature and can be premium, requiring real money purchases. In this case, the more desirable goods would be of higher rarity. This can be useful from the designer's perspective, as within their design documents, they would specify a guideline for the rarities to artists, who would then proceed to create cosmetic items adhering to these rarity guidelines. For example, a legendary premium cosmetic would come with all sorts of additional features like special visual effects.

Unlike real-world goods which naturally deteriorate over time and lose their value, digital goods tend to retain their value, although the games themselves become dated. The rarity systems, when built in tandem with a progression system, have a tendency to force some degree of obsolescence onto the items the player acquires. More details on this particular property of rarities are covered in Chapter 5.

Skill Trees

Typically an element found in role-playing games, a skill tree provides a creative solution for designers to integrate the increase of a character's abilities into the progression system.

Skill trees are typically composed of a series of abilities, which can be acquired in succession via some type of special currency, such as skill points (potentially laid out in the user interface as a series of vertices and edges, a graph from discrete mathematics). In this case, players would gain skill points through gameplay and spend them to unlock the skills.

The concept of skills can be adapted to fit different genres and may appear under different names specific to a game's lore. Some examples of skills in this context might be quicker regeneration of lost health, or a longer time for a character to hold their breath underwater.

While the basic form remains, there are many complexities that can be added to this design, depending on the requirements of the project. It may be the case that the skills are unlocked, but only a limited number of skills can be equipped at any one time, creating strategic depth to the metagame.

Perks

A perk within video games refers to some type of bonus or power-up which can be equipped. They have some relation to skills, but are typically provided to characters, weapons or similar gameplay elements in all of which they can be seen as an additional, complementing component. For example, a weapon within a first-person shooter game may come with a slot for a perk to be equipped, and the perk could be an increase in the speed at which the weapon transitions from hip-fire to aiming down sights.

While perks would mainly fall under the system design umbrella, the economy designer will be a stakeholder since perks as a concept can be used to provide new layers of depth and utility to existing content. They can feed into the content-specific progression tracks and give players new strategies. As an example of an alternative application of perks, they could be used to provide uniqueness and variability to weapons and equipment, being randomly applied to the weapon as a bonus. Perks are a useful metagame tool to be used creatively by designers.

Design Challenges and Theoretical Considerations for the Economy Designer

Pacing of Content

The progression system provides the key means of controlling the rate at which content is made available to the player, but the balancing and manipulation of this by the game economy designer is the key to making sure content is delivered to players in a sufficient, but not excessive quantity.

Game economy designers often feel the need to keep players interested by allowing access to valuable content, but this can quite easily get out of hand. When working on a game, designers can become too close to the product, and this can distort their perception of the value of the content they are working with. Pressure from other developers on the team, project direction and company management concerned with profit and loss does not always help either. As a result, content can be made too easily available to players. This could be due to the progression system being too forgiving, or sources providing too much currency. Players will burn through this content and be left with nothing to chase, giving little reason to keep returning to the game.

Conversely, there is the problem of moving too far in the opposite direction and balancing the game's economy systems in such a way that content is not provided quickly enough. Essentially, in this case you are preventing a player from seeing new features and/or items. There is a loose parallel with the trends in difficulty curves of games which changed as the industry evolved. Why spend a lot of money creating expensive-to-produce story cutscenes if only a few players are going to see them?

From my experience, the risk of burning content is the easier trap to fall into, given that it is more noticeable via calculation, spreadsheet simulation and general feel if something is out of reach, than if it is too close to require substantial effort to attain.

Fungibility and Divisibility

Fungibility is a term from economics which refers to the ability of a good to be interchanged with another good of the same type. For example, in the real world, a $100 bill is fungible as it can be replaced with another $100 bill, which has the same value. However, a valuable painting is not fungible, as it is unique and cannot simply be exchanged for another valuable painting having the exact same meaning and quality to a person.

This is a fairly straightforward theory, but certainly one which the game economy designer should be aware of. The concept of Non-Fungible Tokens giving birth to a new subset of the games industry is a separate topic. For this section, I am considering the fundamental impact the theory has on high-level game economy design.

To cite one example, at times the concept of resources and currencies become interwoven during design, even if simply within the language used to communicate with different members of the development team. Fungibility is key to determining the difference. Take the game *Marvel Snap* as a reference. The game is a collectible card game where the player must upgrade cards by using a soft currency (called credits), along with resources (called boosters) of which there is a specific type for each card. In this context, the credits are fungible, and the boosters are non-fungible, with both required in order to upgrade a card, giving birth to the entire system of long-term player engagement. A card can be upgraded via the boosters, which must be obtained by playing the game with that card. There is some player choice involved in choosing which cards to play to gain boosters for them, but the task of simulating a player's progress for game balancing becomes more predictable with the non-fungibility of the boosters. On the other hand, the fungibility of credits inherently comes with pure player choice as to which cards to focus on upgrading. Within the game this is used cleverly as a "buy around" to circumvent the need for boosters.

Another theoretical case could be the means which are used to determine the success of a player at a particular game. A project I worked on involved minor discussions about modifying the core experience to incentivize players to attain a high score, with currency as the reward, which would have been an ineffective route to take. A reward in the form of a currency cannot be thought of as a high score, as a currency is (often) fungible, but a high score is not. While a high score may come with a material reward, in real life as well as in video games, the very thought of attaining a world number one score at any game, then exchanging this for a material reward, but losing the world number one score in the process, is relatively absurd.

Related to fungibility is the idea of *divisibility*, whereby typically a currency can be divided into smaller units without the loss of value (e.g. Ten $10 bills equals one $100 bill). Within games this is utilized effectively for giving out different currency rewards for the various player engagements and actions. The average amount of a main soft currency should be given out in relatively large quantities, for example with base 1000. This means that you have the freedom to give smaller or larger rewards to players. For example, an average payout can be several thousand for completing a standard main mission or match, with higher rewards for better performing players, but also much smaller quantities for retention mechanisms, such as daily logins. There is flexibility in the amounts that can be given, but starting with a smaller base value would limit this flexibility, as the units cannot be subdivided, which in turn can back the designer into a corner with no viable rewards to give players.

On the other hand, this is not to say that having a smaller base value does not serve a purpose. It will give the currency more value to players and can effectively be used as a rare, end-game currency tailored to specific purposes within the game.

Player Planning and Depth: Optimization

One of the beautiful characteristics of video games is the variety of experiences they can offer. Certain games lay out everything for the player with clear rulesets and strive for symmetry. They are typically designed for competitive multiplayer gameplay. Other games interweave stories into the gameplay and are designed to be enjoyed by the solo player. The interesting aspect which covers both of these greatly differing types of games is the ability to give the player deviations from their main path of progression and/or learning during their overall lifetime with the product. A way of looking at this is that there must be some degree of uncertainty within the player's engagement, and players must be able to develop their own strategies while playing, optimizing their way through the economy. In simple terms, there must be the capacity for a player to feel like they are "winning", beyond the core gameplay and into economy systems. Finding a middle ground solution to these two rather contradictory aims is the ultimate goal for the designer when constructing the meta systems. In one instance, a well-balanced economy (which is easier to simulate and ultimately control) is one in which every player has an approximately similar experience: similar resources, time for progression, etc. However, with this approach, there is inherently little capacity for players to find an optimal path and stand out from one another. We need to be able to make players feel intelligent by adding more depth and the capacity for mastery. This is naturally very easy to say in theory, but much more difficult to achieve in practice, however much the designer might see it as the ultimate goal for a game. An approach which is considered best practice would be to keep the behavior and state of the economy heavily controlled and even contrived, early on in the player's journey, but as the player progresses and invests more time into the game, this control must be released as players get deeper into the systems. At this point our economy modeling should show more deviations from the main path, more extreme situations and the potential for the top small percentage of players to find themselves in unique positions relative to the main player base (Figure 2.4).

To help us in creating an economy which has a blend of keeping players on the same path while allowing optimization, we should consider deterministic and non-deterministic properties. A game will have deterministic properties, whereby the player will gain clear knowledge in advance of the rewards they are going to receive. Typical deterministic properties are the core rewards from repeated engagement with the game, which can take different forms. A good example would be the soft currency rewards that a player gains from playing the individual matches or battles within a PvP game, or the rewards from daily challenges. Players will begin to get a feel for these rewards

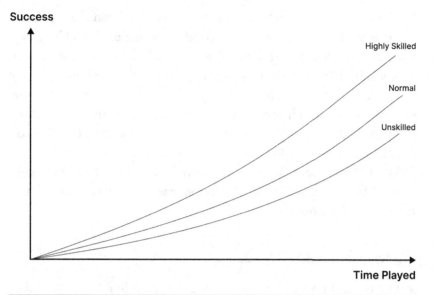

Figure 2.4   Graph showing general success versus time played for different player skill levels.

and how they contribute to the progression and game content. They will attain the knowledge that if they play X number of daily missions to receive in-game cash, they will be able to buy a cheap upgrade to a weapon.

Deterministic rewards can be abstract and extend to different things such as new story beats and chapters within a narrative driven title, depending on how this is presented to the player. Deterministic rewards are a necessary component to help establish a regular habit among players, but a game consisting only of deterministic rewards will become extremely predictable and quickly become an experience revolving around grinding. Some grind can be enjoyable, but in excess this can become detrimental to the game overall.

To complement deterministic rewards, we also combine their use with non-deterministic properties. These are unpredictable, random, rare and surprising rewards or characteristics within the game economy. Examples of non-deterministic rewards include rare loot drops from boss characters, or aspects of the end-game content containing powerful properties. Non-deterministic rewards inject a level of uncertainty and interest for the player, they provide the aforementioned deviations and also breathe life into the game economy's capacity to provide optimization for the most engaged and skilled players.

There exists a synergy between deterministic and non-deterministic rewards, and both are required. The effect of one tends to bleed into the other. We can get a feel for the regular cadence of rewards that are deterministic, but we can also use these rewards to potentially save for some rare event. For example, a player may gain regular rewards from daily missions, which they can either spend on common content, or can potentially be saved to eventually purchase a loot box, which has the chance to give a rare reward.

With the properties discussed above, we can craft an intricately balanced economy which appeals to the mass player base, but also has the potential for mastery.

Player Frustration and the Possibility of Failure

While frustration may be seen as a negative emotion, the truth is that all games need to feature an amount of frustration as part of their overall experience, otherwise they will not hold the player's interest. Frustration derives from failing a certain section of gameplay or becoming unable to proceed due to the inability to solve a problem. The game economy must also play on this emotion.

The game economy must have the capacity for player failure at times. Put another way, the idea of success and failure, which is a fundamental driver for almost every game, must also be present within the game economy.

Normally, games will feature optimal paths through the economy for the top percentage of players, and likewise sub-optimal paths for unskilled players, though the trajectory will typically remain in a positive direction. Some basic rewards for pure time investment are beneficial, but it must also be true that certain things should be unattainable for all but the most dedicated players.

Complexity, Confusion and Player Focus

Inevitably, during the development of a game project, things will become overwhelming, both in terms of the workload but also in terms of the designed systems and the supporting tools, settings, spreadsheets and documentation. Game economy is especially at risk of developing into overwhelming complexity.

As you work on and build out the game economy, you will develop an expanding spreadsheet simulation of these intertwining systems. It is very easy to lose sight of the initial goal or vision when working deep into a mathematical model of a game economy. It is also likely that at times during the project you will find yourself sidetracked, and when revisiting the game economy model it will be so convoluted that it will be prohibitively difficult to get back into the flow of understanding your own methods.

A way to mitigate this is to maintain your own notes, either within the spreadsheet or within a separate document which explains each part of the simulation and its purpose. This may seem like common sense, but during the throes of development when you are extremely busy, it can become easy to cut corners and forego small steps such as these.

As with many aspects of life in general, the adage "keep it simple, stupid" is something to bear in mind. When faced with different approaches, the simplest approach is highly likely to be the most effective. Complexity will inevitably come along of its own accord.

Writing down and attempting to explain the problem you are trying to solve can help a great deal, as is trying to teach this to another person. It is a good idea to find a co-worker and run them through the system as a sanity check, and if you find that you cannot explain this to them or teach them how something is intended to work, recognize that it is already too complex.

Related to the issues of losing track of the vision when working with spreadsheet simulations, is the idea of losing track of the sense of player enjoyment within a game economy. This is potentially a sensitive topic in the field of game design. Following best practices and pure game economy theory is naturally something which you should aim to do, but remember that a spreadsheet simulation will not tell you about the general sense of fun while playing a game. A game can be very well balanced but still not enjoyable to the player, and by extension the metagame can be economically strong but still not fun to play. Different factors cause that unquantifiable "fun" aspect for different games.

Naturally, it is still important to playtest the game and work in close collaboration with other system designers during the development cycle. However, this is where a contradiction can arise. As the game economy, progression and all meta-related systems concern themselves with the long-term engagement of players, it is – in theory – highly inefficient, if not impossible to personally playtest these features. How would one test a feature which is designed to be experienced by players over months of engagement, as opposed to seconds or minutes? Emotionally, it is also extremely difficult to put yourself into the position of the player for meta systems, as you are building the game and naturally will never experience the true value of the content as if you were a real end user. In other words, long-term engagement systems do not lend themselves to the concept of prototyping; building, testing, iterating in quite the same way as core action phase gameplay. Therefore, we do need to rely on theory more often, and with experience, we begin to get a feel for what works and what does not. That being said, it is still possible to test out the fun factor with the team by establishing a close working relationship with other designers and having the appropriate debug tools to allow quickened progression. This is a difficult theoretical reality to work around, but is again a good reason to keep things simple initially and then work in potential complexities later in the process. This mitigates the risk of a convoluted system which loses sight of the enjoyment it is designed to create.

The Endowment Effect

The endowment effect is an emotional bias which causes individuals to place a greater value on things that they own, beyond the recognized market value of those things. In other words, if you own something, you will tend to place more value on it just from the notion of owning it, compared to the value you would place on the same thing if you did not own it. The endowment effect is a well-recognized concept from Behavioural Economics and extends far beyond video games. It is the endowment effect which causes people to hold onto items as opposed to selling them, even when they would be in a position to make a profit from the sale. For example, someone who buys an expensive bottle of whisky could be offered the chance to sell at a higher price years later, but will be inclined to hold onto it due to the endowment effect, despite the notable financial benefits from selling.

I consider this theory to be a useful tool in the economy designer's arsenal. Beyond the rather trivial notion of giving items to players, which is a natural occurrence in many games, how could you make a more creative use of the endowment effect? For games with randomly dropped rewards, there are opportunities. For example, a game may contain a reward chest that has a rarity (either Common, Uncommon, Rare, Epic or Legendary) associated with it. A Rare Chest would typically contain items which are also of the Rare rarity and possibly some items which are of a lower Uncommon rarity; positive surprises do not mean much if there are no negative surprises to go along with them! However, considering this, the Rare Chest may be implemented with a small chance of dropping an item which is of the higher Epic rarity. A player who gets this item will suddenly own a higher value item than they would expect, and the endowment effect will add a greater sense of worth to the item. This can have a positive impact on player engagement and retention in the long term.

Marvel: Contest of Champions is a fighting game, but centers around collecting characters via randomly generated reward drops. I noticed that when playing, relatively early on within this game I ended up owning a single character of a much higher rarity than others in my collection. For this free-to-play title, where my user account essentially required no initial payment, suddenly owning this character gave my account a higher value. For this contextually small early reward, I felt a better connection to this game and more drive to keep playing.

The Peak-End Rule

The Peak-End Rule is a psychological heuristic which relates to how we reflect on past experiences. Rather than recalling these experiences based on an average of the positive and negative moments, according to the Peak-End Rule we tend to remember these experiences with opinions heavily influenced by the most intense point and the end point. This is something which we observe and experience in many walks of life. An example relates to the level of pain two patients experience during a medical procedure. Even if the procedure is longer for one patient, and therefore this patient experiences an overall higher average level of pain, the procedure will be remembered as worse by the other patient who had a shorter procedure but with a more painful ending and possibly a more intense peak of pain at some point along the way. The Peak-End Rule can apply to both positive and negative experiences, but it must be noted that there is another psychological heuristic which comes into play here: *The Negativity Bias.* This states that negative experiences tend to be more impactful on people than positive experiences, even if they are both of the same degree of respective intensities. If follows that when applied to the Peak-End Rule, a negative experience will hold a degree of dominance whether at the peak or at the end, and a positive experience would need to be significantly more intense than a negative one to overcome and influence one's subsequent reflections or memories.

How can this be applied within video game design? There are many possibilities. It is one reason why the climax of a story-driven game must be strong. It is common to hear developers talk extensively about catching player's attention at the beginning of a game to prevent early churn, but in this context, the exit point for the player at the end of the game is what they will take away from it.

On the opposite side of player experience is a casual game, where the designer can incorporate the Peak-End Rule into specific player rewards given to the player after a typical play session, such as a special reward for playing a certain number of successive matches in a multiplayer game, giving the player the chance to leave their current play session on a high note.

Storytelling and Narrative Considerations

Often the notion of game economy and the entire collection of features related to the metagame is pigeonholed as being the necessary evil and perhaps the more tedious area of game design. Personally, I find this to be misguided as it often runs in tandem with the notion that there is an excessive amount of extremely open-ended creativity involved in game design. Realistically, game design is about problem solving, with elements of creativity, which are essentially a type of creative problem solving. There are certainly times when there is a kernel of truth to the boring side of game design, and if you find yourself in a position where you are manually designing particular engagement features such as a multitude of gameplay challenges (think along the lines of "killing X enemies to get Y rewards"), you may agree that this can become relatively thankless. However, you will generally find that similarly banal tasks come with every aspirational career or professional practice, so game design is no different in this respect.

But what about the meta-related features themselves? Will these become uninteresting to players as they exist to maintain engagement, provide content and form habits, but do not truly add to the enjoyment?

Naturally, in an ideal world, the suspension of disbelief should be maintained as much as possible throughout a player's lifetime with a game. Therefore, somehow tying everything to the lore and narrative is important. It could be said that this is not really the job of the game economy designer, but you will need to work with the narrative team to achieve this wholly desirable outcome. This is one of many necessary collaborations during a project, and gaining an understanding of storytelling and the methods of the narrative designers and writers will undoubtedly help you as economy designer.

Of course, some genres lend themselves to narrative more than others; single player action adventure or interactive drama games give extensive focus to the narrative and the designers can find more creative ways to tie the economy to this.

The connection to narrative for game economy can go much further. While speaking to a colleague during a past project, the discussion moved toward what makes a specific game economy fun to play. This may be an odd thought in itself, but very relevant in the sense that the player must be able to play the game economy just like they play the core gameplay (albeit never in quite the same sense). A starting point would be the narrative framing for the game economy. A fly-by-night black market with piracy and other crimes is inherently going to have a fun factor and a type of tension that a regular market would find very difficult to achieve. This is just one example, but depending on the project, it would be an important consideration when fleshing out the game concept along with the lore.

The platform and business model come into play here, and with free-to-play mobile games there will typically be more blatant meta features designed to boost retention and other key metrics, and the necessity for tying these to the narrative in interesting ways may not be something that is a core part of the project. Nevertheless, for many games, the limits lie in creativity itself, and it is my personal belief that this is an area where there is untapped potential for innovation.

References

Call of Duty: Modern Warfare, Activision, 2019

Deconstructor of Fun, 2012. https://www.deconstructoroffun.com/blog

Game Balance (first edition), Ian Schreiber & Brendas Romero, 2022

Game Design: Theory and Practice (second edition), Richard Rouse III, 2005

Game Wisdom: Theories on Game Design, "Debating Difficulty Curves in Game Design", 2021. https://game-wisdom.com/critical/debating-difficulty-game-design

Gameplay and Design, Kevin Oxland, 2004

Make Use Of, "11 Ways Progression Works in Video Games", 2022. https://www.makeuseof.com/video-game-progression-ways

PositivePsychology.com, "What is the Peak-End Rule? How to Use it Smartly", 2019. https://positivepsychology.com/what-is-peak-end-theory

Thinking, Fast and Slow, Daniel Kahneman, 2011

3

Processes, Design Skills and Development Strategies

A key vision point for this book is the idea of a practical approach that you can utilize directly within whatever projects you are working on. This chapter details the actual work that you will undertake during the project, complete with examples and the skills and techniques required.

Starting with documentation, the chapter moves onto working with spreadsheets for game economy modeling, with some standard examples that underpin many game economy features. These contain methods which form a foundation and can be actively built upon. From this design phase, the chapter gives some insight into the practicalities of moving a designed system into the game, working together with programmers and other disciplines. To round things off, I have covered some useful foundational mathematical skills.

The Game Design Document

The game design document is a key component of development. In this section I will cover the format and content of a game design document from the game economy designer's perspective.

Structure

Often, when reading about a game design document there will be many books, websites, guides and other sources pertaining to game design education that will highlight the concept of a game design bible, a single game design document describing all features in detail. This can be a moment of enlightenment for any graduate or junior designer thinking through everything that constitutes the game.

DOI: 10.1201/9781003386865-4

While the exact amount of detail put into documentation is debated among designers, it would be true to say that it is essential to be able to record information in a written format. With experience you start to know what works and what doesn't, and with a large team, you do need some type of written direction. Ideas are easily forgotten if not written down. Even if a game design document does not feel necessary, I can assert from personal experience that it definitely is. An idea in the mind is vague and meaningless but once it is written down, it is inherently broken down into its core building blocks in a more systematic way. If you are struggling to write it down in a concise format, this suggests that there are flaws that need to be addressed.

There is also the myth that there is a single format for a game design document, used as an industry standard. This is not true. The nature of the game design document will vary dramatically depending on the genre, scope and studio working on the game. A document for a small indie puzzle game will be very different from the document for an AAA action-adventure game, which will in itself also vary greatly from the design document of a sports game.

Nevertheless, if you are to approach writing a design document for a complete game, it would be sensible to include sections on the following:

- High-Level Overview of the Core Gameplay and the unique selling points or hooks for the game
- Game mechanics
- Game elements, including characters, weapons, items and objects
- Details on specific systems within the game
- Artificial intelligence
- User interface
- Art
- Sound
- Story

Even for game economy design, these aspects are interesting and useful to think through, and this type of written direction is something with which you should become familiar. When I was working with my own independent studio, focusing on smaller projects, I found this approach useful with our documentation.

Although it is useful to consider the idea of a holistic single game design document which contains the above sections, in a professional sense, when working with a larger team, this is impractical. The design documents I have worked with generally take the form of a folder containing a repository of smaller documents pertaining to specific features, and offshoots of these features, complemented by spreadsheets, and a multitude of diagrams, files, sketches, mock-ups, special files and many other bespoke materials that are difficult to quantify.

While there may be no single right answer to creating a game design document, it is definitely possible for bad game design documents to be written. For a single document for a feature, again there is no standard format, but there are some best practices which I would recommend following.

The Document Header

As a starting point, I would suggest that the beginning of the document features a top section containing the information detailed below, which can be presented in bullet points under each of the three headings. There are a few key reasons to include this feature at the top of a design document. First, it is important to reinforce the reason for designing the feature. It must have an end goal, more often than not, solving a specific problem or set of problems within the project. When communicating with different team members from different disciplines within the studio, it is effective to begin any conversation by stating what problem you are trying to solve. The design document is an important artifact in facilitating this.

Second, the document may be read by members of the studio from various disciplines or top-down positions within the studio, where knowing the low-level details of the feature is less important, but having a clear idea of what needs to be solved and how this can be solved is sufficient.

Third, including a specification of the telemetry (see Chapter 5) is vital, as this should be built into the feature as part of its main implementation, as opposed to telemetry being included as an afterthought. Therefore, tying this information into the design document helps greatly with the development pipeline.

Goals of the Feature   Here you should concisely and succinctly state what problem this design is trying to solve.

How Will the Feature Achieve These Goals?   You should explain in one or two lines what the feature is going to do in order to achieve these goals defined under the first heading.

Relevant Analytics to Track to Analyze the Feature   List the key metrics that you are hoping to improve with the feature (e.g. Retention), but also the feature-specific data you believe would be helpful to track to improve the feature in the long term.

Main Document Content

The actual structure within these feature documents is, as mentioned, subjective. As a general starting point, I use the following sections within the majority of my documents, and some may be further divided into subsections. As always with game design, there are no universal standards and nothing is set in stone. Use the following points as a guideline only.

An Overview of the Feature

This section is the creative overview of the feature. I like to keep these relatively short and would consider using bullet points to show the most important parts of the feature. This section may include a subsection containing the look and feel of the feature, if it is for a large, narratively connected aspect to the game. A synopsis is a short form of a longer text, summarizing only the important points. The term can also involve taking a longer, detailed piece of text such as a novel and summarizing it into several key paragraphs. This is also a very useful skill for a designer, and it is something that can and should be practiced and improved. It will be highly relevant to many aspects of the game design role, in various contexts other than writing design documents.

How It Works

This section is the core of the document, including all the relevant information which will be read by other designers and team members from different disciplines – mainly art and programming – necessary to implement the feature. This section may include several subsections and itself can become quite extensive. If this section becomes overly long-winded, it might be worth considering separating the feature into multiple documents.

An Example Calculation or Procedure

This section involves showing an example of the particular feature in a practical sense within the game. Although not all features – including economy related features – involve numerical calculations, showing something in the context of the game you are building is very powerful. I have found many hundreds of ways to describe the way things work, yet there are still different ways to interpret the information. I have also had some tough career moments trying to convey complex mechanics which caused issues with misinterpreted designs. The way in which you can show examples varies, but whenever arithmetic is involved within the design, aim to illustrate it in action with relevant numbers. If you have studied either physics or mathematics in high school or beyond, you may remember being taught a new concept and being given worked examples to follow. You then are given similar problems to solve that expand on these examples. As a very rough, simplified example, let's say you are working on the design of an experience point progression system for a first-person shooter game. Weapons increase their level based on playing player-versus-player matches, with the amount of experience points awarded being modified based on player performance. Completing the match gives a set base amount of experience points to the weapon. Each kill gives a defined amount of experience points, and there is a headshot multiplier for each kill.

The base amount is defined as 200 experience points. Each kill awards 50 experience points, and the headshot multiplier is 20% extra.

The player finishes a match with "Assault Rifle A" equipped, getting 13 normal kills and 4 headshot kills.

Therefore, the experience points the player gets for "Assault Rifle A" is:

$$200 + 13 * 50 + 4 * 50 * 1.20 = 1090$$

This type of example removes potential ambiguity for the programmer implementing the system, but also for yourself who may be called upon to revisit the system months later after working on a different area. It will help you to recall the specific method you previously designed. Worked examples can also help to highlight pitfalls within a design.

User Interface Considerations   Depending on the feature, this section can be optional. Including a basic mock-up screen (below) can be sufficient. There may be other information related to the user interface which would be useful to include and you can also include references to other games as a guideline.

Basic Mock-up(s)   "A picture is worth a thousand words". Although I consider this to be optional, some features can benefit from the designer putting together a basic visual mock-up, just to clarify what the designer has in their mind when writing the document. Depending on the studio, an artist may have time to help in this respect. However, if you happen to be able to throw together some simple visuals with whatever resources you have, then this is certainly not a bad thing. As a child, I used to draw constantly, but I do not consider myself to have any artistic ability relative to video game art. Art ability is not essential when it comes to game economy design, but if you can show something mocked up in *MS Paint*, or with the shape presets on *Google Slides*, this can be helpful.

Narrative/Lore Context   This section can be seen as optional, and some economy and meta-related features will be more connected to the narrative than others. From my personal approach, I have always tended to draw a separation between the systemic design – including economy – and the narrative design. One discipline interfering with another can create problems, and these will naturally happen without the need to exacerbate them. When working on a project, you will find that it's best to use common sense and collaborate where necessary with narrative designers. A game economy should ideally be engaged with, and part of, the suspension of disbelief, so working with the narrative team will be inevitable at times. For this section, you can add a little narrative flavor related to the feature. You could include short descriptions of how your design ties in to the overarching story and theme of the game and potentially some information about how the feature behaves, which can be justified by the narrative.

Detail Level Summary

The level of detail within a design document may be variable. Again, this relates to the genre, studio and scope, but more importantly the area of the game that the document is covering. Narrative-related documents can be more descriptive, but for system and economy design, the document can be more mathematical in nature and will comprise more bullet points, tables, etc. Overly ambiguous statements can be problematic. A prime example from my personal experience on a project involved a key design vision for a competitive multiplayer title, that stated: "The game must be easy to get into, but have the perception of mastery". This is essentially defining an ideal game, but there is absolutely nothing for the designer to work on.

On the other hand, there is the document that is too detailed, covering every last detail of a feature. This is a potential trap for game designers and although there are varying degrees of "too much detail", it can be detrimental to a game for several reasons. First, there is no real way of knowing the exact details of a game at the documentation stage, and this information will largely become redundant later on. One prime example is balancing values. I do not believe actual numbers of this kind have any place in a game design document. This is why we have spreadsheets. In a game design document, if the designer is specifying balancing values, it would be far more prudent to simply specify what the balancing values (or variables) are and then use spreadsheet simulation and/or special software tools or the game engine editor to specify actual numbers. This point should not be confused with example calculations or mock-ups within the document, which of course can use numbers to show the designer's intentions.

Other reasons to steer clear of too much detail within a document are that it will become more confusing for the reader, and finally, documents quickly become outdated, and the more specific details there are, the more they will become irrelevant in due course. This will leave the designer to spend more arduous hours updating the document at various points during development.

When working with other team members from the programming and art departments, it is important for these individuals to take the document and scrutinize it from their own standpoint. In many cases, there should be technical documentation and art style guides or similar created by people from these specializations. These take inspiration from the design document and run in tandem.

Sample Document for a Game Feature

Included here is an example game design document for a metagame and economy-related feature for Project X, the hypothetical free-to-play, player-versus-player, first-person shooter video game detailed in the previous chapter. I have chosen to include a design for a system of daily and weekly missions that the player can undertake as part of the engagement and retention drivers.

Feature Design Document Example: Daily and Weekly Missions

Heading Section

Goals of the Feature
- To boost retention
- To help drive monetization via the Battle Pass feature
- To drive a regular habit of engaging with the game, coaxing players to return

How Will the Feature Achieve These Goals?
- The feature will provide a series of intrinsic challenges for the player to perform, providing regular rewards.
- The feature will keep the challenges rotating on a daily and weekly basis to coax a habit from the player.
- The weekly missions will assist progression through the Battle Pass tiers.

Relevant Analytics to Track to Analyze the Feature
- Retention
- Conversion Rate and Average Revenue per Daily Active User
- Which daily missions are completed most out of the master pool of missions
- Which weekly missions are completed most out of the master pool of missions

- The average number of matches played to complete daily and weekly missions
- Average hard currency spend associated with the weekly missions

Main Section

Overview   The daily and weekly missions for Project X are composed of challenges that the player can attempt and complete. A challenge is a specifically defined thing to do within the game, giving the player a reward.

The daily and weekly missions are accessed from their own screen on the main menu, with a user interface showing missions that are available, their associated rewards and a representation of the player's progress on missions currently available.

Daily missions are available for all players to undertake and complete, without the need for microtransactions, and present the player with small contributions to Battle Pass progression. These challenges are designed to be easily repeatable, so the same daily missions can become available on subsequent days.

Weekly missions are chiefly tied to the Battle Pass, which runs in seasons of two months, and involve a set of challenges for the player to complete each week. Each subsequent week, a new set of missions is added, so the existing pool of missions expands. Players who purchase the Battle Pass gain access to additional missions each week.

How It Works   The daily missions function as follows:

- Daily missions are simple challenges which the player can complete within one or two sessions, within a single day of play.
- Daily missions have a 24-hour timer, rotating on a daily basis.
  - Daily missions reset at 00.00 UTC.
  - All daily missions are replaced when the reset occurs, regardless of whether the player is in-progress with the mission or not.
- Daily missions are selected from a pool of missions, defined by the designer.

- Daily missions are designed in general to be repeatable. Therefore, the new missions presented each day can be random, automatic selections from the pool of missions.
- There will be N [TBD between 3 & 5] missions selected to appear each day.
- The daily missions will award the player with small amounts of Battle Pass Experience Points and Weapon Research Tokens.

There will be a "meta" daily mission which will be simply for the player to complete all other daily missions.

The meta daily mission will award the player with a small consumable item to be used during a match.

The weekly missions function as follows:

- Weekly missions are given to the player in sets, with a new set being presented to the player each week. A weekly set will contain N number of missions [TBD].
- Each week, a new set will be added with the previous set remaining present, so the overall pool of available missions continually expands each week.
- Weekly missions work with the Battle Pass season. At the start of a season, the first set of weekly missions is unlocked, and then each subsequent week a new set is unlocked until the final week of the Battle Pass season.
- A single set of weekly missions will include some easy missions, some medium difficulty missions and some hard missions:
  - Easy missions can be completed by playing a single match.
  - Medium missions can be completed by playing, for example, 2–3 matches, or require a small amount of repeated practice of certain actions within the game.
  - Hard missions can be completed by playing, for example, 4–6 matches, or require moderate repeated practice at certain actions within the game.
- Weekly missions reward the player primarily with Battle Pass Experience Points and (potentially) some Weapon Research Tokens.
- Each set of weekly missions will include N amount [TBD] of special Premium Weekly Missions. These missions will become available to the player only if they purchase the Battle Pass.

Examples   Examples of daily missions:

"Complete a single match"
"Kill 5 enemies"

Examples of weekly missions:

"Win 10 Matches"
"Attain 50 headshot kills with an Assault Rifle"

User Interface Considerations   Daily missions must be presented to the player in a way that is clear from the main menu, but not too obtrusive. The player must be made aware of new daily missions after running the game for the first time each day. After a daily mission is complete, this must be conveyed to the player on the user interface widget showing the mission. There will be a progress bar that fills up as daily missions are completed, all the way to the meta mission, where the reward will be highlighted to the player.

Weekly missions will be listed on their own screen, accessed from the main menu. The screen will list sets of weekly missions, pertaining to each week of the Battle Pass season. Sets which are not yet available will appear as locked, with a timer showing how long remains until the set unlocks. For each set, the premium weekly missions will also appear locked, with messaging showing that the player must buy the Battle Pass to unlock. This could also act as a link to the Battle Pass screen.

Basic Mock-ups   Figures 3.1 and 3.2 show a basic mock-up of the UI representation showing how a weekly mission will appear within its set.

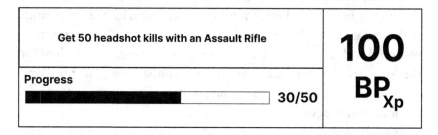

Figure 3.1   Image mock-up of the UI element for a weekly mission in an FPS game.

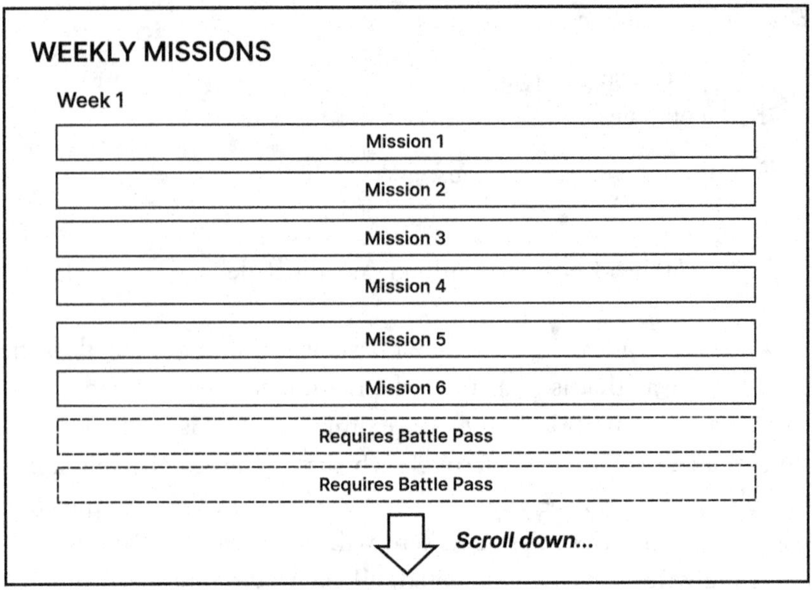

Figure 3.2 Basic mock-up for the UI for a list of weekly missions within an FPS game.

Spreadsheets

On numerous occasions throughout my career, I have been told that the game designer's best friend is the spreadsheet. Spreadsheets are an invaluable tool to make the designer's life easier. They allow information to be arranged in a clear fashion, and they facilitate calculations and analysis. While I believe there is a place for the use of spreadsheets within many design disciplines, for the economy designer I would say that they are essential. For designers concerned with minute-to-minute gameplay, it is necessary for them to take an empirical approach and playtest their systems, refining them into their most enjoyable form. Playtesting and refining to find the fun within a system is also undeniably useful for the economy designer, but with the very nature of the metagame and economy features, it does not tell you everything you need to know in order to keep players engaged. To understand the long-term behavior of your systems, you will need to find some way to model the behavior of the player. This is where the spreadsheet becomes invaluable.

Spreadsheets are immensely complex software programs, and a full breakdown of the extensive features of spreadsheets is beyond the scope of this book. I would go so far as to say that for economy design you will use only a portion of the functionality that spreadsheets provide, although for modeling metagame systems, the level of complexity can rapidly increase. For more information on the detailed use of spreadsheets, there is a vast number of online resources and I would encourage you to look into these.

Some of the ways in which you will use spreadsheets are for tracking content to be planned and implemented into the game, such as lists of premium cosmetic items to go into the store. You may use spreadsheets for task tracking and various other inter-departmental communication reasons. However, the main use of spreadsheets is for the modeling of game economy features. This involves extensive number crunching and often relies on the important random number generation that is part of spreadsheet programs.

This following section covers the common functions and formulas you will find in different spreadsheet programs. You can also use Google to find specific syntax for different spreadsheet software, if necessary. Mainly, the functionality is shared across different programs.

If you are already familiar with spreadsheets, this section will seem extremely facile, but it will progress to something more taxing. I feel it may be helpful to start from the absolute beginning, so that we can move on to the kind of spreadsheet modeling which will take more effort from someone with little basic knowledge.

A spreadsheet is a table of cells, with the columns being referred to as letters and with the rows being numbered (Table 3.1).

With values entered into the cells, the essence of spreadsheets lies in the use of formulas for processing, analyzing and visualizing the data. In order to use formulas, type the "=" sign into any cell, and this will tell the software that a formula is going to be entered into the cell.

Table 3.1 Mock-up of the Appearance of a Spreadsheet

	A	B	C
1			
2			
3			
4			
5			

Following entering the "=" sign into the cell, you then type the name of the formula, with parentheses after to contain the parameters which the formula accepts.

For example, a formula would be:

$$= \text{SUM}(A1 : A20)$$

There are many different formulas within spreadsheet programs, and they all tend to have descriptive names: SUM, COUNT, to name a few. The basic mathematical operators are also used within spreadsheets, which are +, -, *, /, ^, that is addition, subtraction, multiplication, division and exponentiation, respectively.

For example, if there are values in cells A1, A2, A3, you can add up the values here. In cell A4, you could enter =A1 + A2 + A3 which will give the summation of the values in A1, A2 and A3.

The following are some popular formulas that you will encounter in spreadsheet programs.

SUM

The sum formula can be used to achieve the same effect as adding up numbers by simply typing in the "+" operator. The sum formula adds up the values within a series of cells specified by the user.

RAND

This formula generates a random number between 0 and 1. This function is unique in that it does not accept any additional arguments and just needs empty parentheses following it: "()". You will find that this formula is one of the most relevant for building simulations relating to game economy and metagame. Even beyond the design of game features such as random reward drops, finding ways to model hypothetical player behavior itself revolves around random number generation.

RANDBETWEEN

This formula generates a random integer between the two endpoint numbers specified (inclusive) in the parameters of the function. For example, RANDBETWEEN(1,10) would generate a random integer between 1 and 10 inclusive.

VLOOKUP

This formula is used to retrieve specific information from a table and is a very useful function for game economy simulations. There are related functions such as the LOOKUP and HLOOKUP, which should also be researched and utilized. The VLOOKUP accepts four parameters in the following form:

= VLOOKUP(*lookup value, lookup table, column index, type of match*)

The *lookup value* is the value you are trying to find. The formula will check for this value within the first column of the table.

The *lookup table* is the table of values within which the formula will try to find the lookup value (the first column), and then return the target value from another column, specified by the column index.

Therefore, the *column index* is the column number within the table from which to retrieve the target value.

The *type of match* parameter tells the function whether to look for an approximate or an exact match.

Building Spreadsheet Simulations

With the basic principles underpinning spreadsheets covered, this brings us onto the idea of using spreadsheets for the initial stages of planning out a design. The use of spreadsheets follows on from the game design document, but can also work in parallel. You will have a design documented and referenced along the way while building your spreadsheet, and we can now try to bring these together holistically to go through a simple spreadsheet model for a feature.

The specific modeling techniques are dependent on the game that you are creating, but certain best practices exist, and as many systems are shared across different games with only minor alterations, there are general models built with spreadsheets which will be reusable. In fact, within the high-level field of problem solving, be it within game development, programming, engineering, or any related field, when coming across a new problem, recalling a previous situation where you solved a similar problem and reapplying the method is absolutely a viable strategy.

With this in mind, I have chosen two commonly re-usable mechanics to demonstrate how spreadsheets can be used for economy and metagame design: *Account Level Progression* and *Random Drops*. I believe these form a solid foundation for further learning, from which many more complex and related features can be modeled.

Account Level Progression

The first example is the modeling of a simple account leveling up system, as part of a more expansive progression system design. Players gain a number of experience points from gameplay, and this controls their progress through the account levels of the game. I deem this to be an important shared feature across many games, and a foundation for spreadsheet modeling which can be used, reused and built upon to create far more complex and tailored simulations for different projects.

We come back to our example Project X which involves the player engaging in player-versus-player matches in order to gain experience points, causing their account level to increase. Playing matches generates experience points for the player. The amount of experience points gained has a number of determining factors.

The game will contain 51 account levels (0–50), and the designer will define how many experience points are required to reach each account level. From a fresh install, all players begin at level 0 and progress from here by playing matches. This can be represented as a table, which will be defined within the spreadsheet simulation, and then used as part of that simulation. It is likely that you will reference this table of values often throughout the development process, sharing it with relevant developers as part of the overall design process and communication (Table 3.2).

Open your spreadsheet program and in column A list the total number of player levels and, within column B, enter the experience points required to reach each level. The experience points required are the key to determining how fast players progress through the game. You can adjust these values, creating larger or smaller gaps between the experience points required to move through the levels, to speed up or slow down a player's progress. Normally, we would expect the early levels to involve a relatively fast progression, with this slowing down the higher the account level reached. This is a natural high-level

Table 3.2 Mock-up of a Spreadsheet Showing Account Levels and the Experience Points Required to Reach Those Levels

	A	B
	ACCOUNT LEVEL	EXPERIENCE POINTS REQUIRED
1	1	100
2	2	300
3	3	600
4	4	1000
5	5	1500
6	6	2100
7	7	2800
8	*...and so on to Player Level 50*	

direction for the pacing of progression, but remember that different games and business models have different requirements. You may want to speed up progression at a certain point where players are likely to churn and create an overall synergy between fast-paced progression and slower progression.

You may, if you have some knowledge of mathematics, observe that the values shown are derived from a mathematical formula related to the *triangular numbers* (see end of this chapter for a much fuller discussion of the usefulness of mathematics in video game design). For the purposes of planning progression, working with simulations, and as a general guide, using a formula is effective and can be used as a gauge if the game in question features a long-drawn-out progression system with many levels. However, in a practical sense, manually entering and manipulating the numbers required for each level is a much stronger work practice. This will prevent the progression system from becoming a "slave" to the formula and allows the designer to create very specific pacing whenever desired. Inevitably, you will need bespoke and detailed control of the values and progression, and this can only be achieved with manual changes. A formula would be very limiting in this sense, and while manually entering numbers will involve a share of brute force work, this is a necessary undertaking for creating a robust leveling-up system.

The next step is to flesh out the actual player simulation using random numbers. The goal of using spreadsheet simulations in this way is to try to gauge how far the average player will progress after different numbers of play sessions and, by extension, time playing the game.

In this case we know that the player gains experience points for playing matches, so it naturally follows that we know the maximum amount attainable for a single match. Using spreadsheets and random numbers we can simulate the average amount of experience points players will get per match. With this information, we can then find out which level the average player will reach after playing a certain number of matches.

First, leave a single column space between the "Account Level" and "Experience Points Required", and in cell D1 enter "Match Number", then underneath enter the numbers 1–100. For the purpose of this example, we are only going to consider the first 100 matches to observe the behavior of the system for a new player, because this is of utmost importance. In reality, for game economy design you will also want to simulate hundreds of matches, even covering the different player types, such as skilled or unskilled players (Table 3.3).

Within cell E2, enter the RANDBETWEEN function to generate a random number between 100 and 200, then drag this down to fill the column. This will copy the function into the cells below, generating a series of random numbers within the defined limits of 100 and 200. This is designed to simulate the amount of experience points the player is generating per match. For the purpose of this example, I have chosen to represent the experience generated in a very simple fashion. Typically, the means of players gaining experience within a game involves a more complex calculation, based on various gameplay-related criteria (possibly involving killing enemies or completing matches as a starting point). It is likely that you will be able to factor this in and represent the amount of experience points generated in a more accurate fashion pertaining to how it functions within the game.

Table 3.3 Spreadsheet Mock-Up for Calculating the Account Level a Player Reaches

D	E	F	G
MATCH NUMBER	EXP PER MATCH	TOTAL EXP	LEVEL REACHED
1	=RANDBETWEEN(100,200)	=E2	
2		=F2 + E3	
3		=F3 + E4	
4			
5			
...and so on to Match Number 100			

However, generating several hundred experience points on average per match played is a sensible starting point. The sizes of number you are dealing with will be manageable. There is room to lessen or increase the amounts of experience points given, to slow down or speed up progress.

The next step is to find the running total of experience points that a player receives from playing successive matches. To begin with, in cell F2, we want to move over the initial experience points generated from the first match played, so in this cell enter =E2, which will move the randomly generated value of the first match from E2 over to F2. This must be here for the summation to work. Next, in cell F3, enter =F2 + E3 and drag this down to fill the column. This is your running total of experience points.

You now know the total amount of experience points that the player is receiving from playing matches and the experience points required to progress through each Account Level, so the final step remains to cross reference these two items of information.

In cell G2 enter the formula =LOOKUP(F2, $B$2:$B$51, $A$2:$A$51) and drag this down to fill the column. Initially this formula may seem daunting, but we can break it down step by step.

F2 is the first parameter and is the value which the function takes in, to be looked up. In this case we are taking in the value within the running total of experience points the player has.

The second parameter, in this case $B$2:$B$51, uses the value in F2 and checks to find this value within the range of B2 to B51, which is where the thresholds of experience points are stored. It is likely that the exact value for total experience points will not be found within the range B2 to B51, but in this case we are relying on some of the default behaviors of the lookup function. It always performs an approximate match, and when it can't find the match, it will return the next smallest value. Concerning the player's need to reach certain threshold values to move up through the Account Levels, this default behavior works for the problem we are trying to solve.

The $symbol is used to lock the cell reference, telling the spreadsheet software to keep this reference the same when you drag down the formula into the cells below within the column. As we are checking the summed experience points against a finite amount of player levels (1–50), locking this cell reference is essential.

The third parameter, $A$2:$A$51, uses the value found within the second parameter to return the result we are looking for: the Account Level the player has reached. The LOOKUP function here returns the value within the range A2 to A51, which corresponds to the value found from the second parameter.

For example, if the player has current total of 620 experience points, and we come back to look at Table 3.2, then the LOOKUP function will take in the value of 620 experience points and look for this value within the Experience Points Required column (column B). It will not find this exact value, but will find the value 600 as the next smallest. The function will finally check the Account Level column (column A) and return the corresponding value of 3.

A small trick to use is to highlight an empty cell and hit the delete key to regenerate random numbers within the spreadsheet. In the case of this example simulation, the experience points generated will change each time, and you will see the "Level Reached" therefore also update. You can imagine each time you regenerate the randomly generated values as representing a playthrough of the game (Table 3.4). It can be useful to generate multiple playthroughs and store this data, to get an overall idea of how the system will behave for many players.

The final piece of insight we will aim to get from this simulation is a measure of the time it takes for players to progress through the levels. Within column G, you should have the levels that have been reached by the player, and in the columns next to this we will add information about the time taken to reach those levels.

Table 3.4 Spreadsheet Mock-Up for Calculating the Player's Time in Game Relevant to Their Account Level

G	H	I	J
LEVEL REACHED	TIME IN GAME (MINS)	TIME IN GAME (HRS)	TIME PER MATCH (MINS)
	=J2	=H2/60	5
	=H2+$J$2	=H3/60	
	=H3+$J$2	=H4/60	
...and so on to Match Number 100			

Coming along to column J, within cell J1 enter the name "Time per Match (mins)" which will be the initial estimate of how long a match takes. This is simply an example, but as the game is built you should be able to gauge how long a match takes, and this is also information you could gain from level designers. For the purpose of this example, enter the value 5 into cell J2.

Next, within cell H1, enter the name "Time in Game (mins)", and then underneath in cell H2 enter =J2, to bring the value 5 across to H2. In cell H3 enter the formula =H2+$J$2 and drag this down to fill the column. This will create a running summation of the time each match takes and shows how long the player spends in matches to reach each level. For hourly playtime, this is handled by column I. This simply takes the value in column H, measured in minutes, and converts them to hours by dividing by 60.

With this relatively simple spreadsheet simulation, you now know approximately how many matches it takes for the player to reach certain Account Levels, along with an estimate of the time in game that this will take. Although the session length will in many circumstances be an approximation – there are exceptions – the act of including this is important. Everyone has different lives, but we all share 24 hours in a day. You should be aiming to balance the amount of resources, currency or goods earned with the time it takes in game. In other words, the rate of resources per unit time is the base line for balancing and controlling.

You can modify the experience points required to reach certain levels, and the progression will speed up or slow down accordingly. By extension, there is the flexibility to adjust the player's rate of progression to suit your needs relevant to the game in question. You may want to consider making certain sections of the progression faster, pushing players through more easily, while making other sections slower and requiring more grind.

If the game has currencies that are attained from the gameplay, a similar simulation can be built concerning the amounts of currency owned by players, and this can work in tandem with this simulation to show the amount of currency owned by players at the different levels.

Going further, if you are going to be distributing certain items or unlocking new game features based on this account level, then you know what items different players have by each level and what they could cost with in-game currency.

This progression system model forms a solid basis for many key metagame modeling tasks, but it is only the starting point. There are also other ways to solve similar problems using other formulas within spreadsheet programs. I would encourage regular practice alongside experimenting with other methods to solve similar problems, and building upon the basics of using random numbers within spreadsheets will allow you to model more complex systems.

Random Reward Drops

We have already covered examples of the use of random numbers within game economy design, and invariably you will find that the use of random numbers occurs on many occasions. Their use can be thought of as yet another tool for the game economy designer to use. Within this second example, we will explore a more direct use of random number generation: one that underpins the concept of random rewards used in many games.

First, the term "gacha" is used to cover the same concept within different contexts in various games. The term derives from "Gachapon", a physical vending machine popular in Japan that dispenses small capsule toys.

Gacha games take this concept and utilize it within video games. A point to note is that the term gacha can be used to refer to a genre of games, revolving around a key mechanic of content collection, usually in the form of hero characters, but gacha can also be used to refer to specific mechanics within games. This is a system within the game designed to allow the player to spend an amount of in-game currency in order to roll a random reward.

The random nature of the rewarded item underpinning the entire concept of gacha requires a system design for distributing the rewards, and this is handled through a "roll table".

The design for a roll table can be put together effectively with a spreadsheet, utilizing more random number generation to simulate roll table behavior. The following spreadsheet model can be re-used in different scenarios to help gauge the behavior of random rewards within many meta and related systems. In this example, fruit represents the items being awarded, but it is useful to think about the wider range of applications for this method. Weapons, cards or character

Table 3.5 Table Showing the Percentage Drop Chance of Different Fruit Items

ITEM	DROP CHANCE (%)
Apple	20
Banana	30
Pear	10
Orange	15
Mango	25

drops across many different genres can be governed by similar random drop methods. Game development is full of a blend of theoretical and practical problems to solve. A point to note is that even if the concept of random rewards is not directly included within your game, you are inevitably going to need to require ways to estimate behavior of hypothetical play-throughs of the game. Using random results to observe patterns within design is going to be relevant, so it is always best to keep an open mind when it comes to game development challenges.

If we think of a roll table as something that you would put into a design document, it would probably take the form of a table similar to Table 3.5, with percentage chances showing the likelihood of a certain item being given to the player.

Our next step is to use spreadsheet software to create a series of mock drops, as if this were a roll table implemented into a game.

Open a blank sheet within your spreadsheet software and within the first cell of columns A, B, C and D enter the names "Chance Value", "Item Name", "Frequency" and "Percentage Chance", respectively, then continue to complete the "Item Name" and "Frequency" columns, as shown in Table 3.6.

Table 3.6 Spreadsheet Mock-Up of the Basis of a Drop Table Simulation

	A	B	C	D
1	CHANCE VALUE	ITEM NAME	FREQUENCY	PERCENTAGE CHANCE
2		N/A	0	
3		Apple	100	
4		Banana	100	
5		Pear	100	
6		Orange	100	
7		Mango	100	
8			=SUM(C2:C7)	

With the sum formula in cell C8, the result in this case appears as 500, adding up the values of the cells from C2 to C7. These values in the "Frequency" column are the numbers that you will manually manipulate to change the "Percentage Chance" values, calculated below. Note that we use the frequency column as a control value, which when changed affects the percentage chance accordingly. The values in the frequency column can be of any number range you choose. For example, you can set each of these to 1000 and the percentage chance generated will be the same. Essentially, there is leeway to allow for fine tuning of the percentage chances. As a starting point, they are set to 100 each.

For the "Percentage Chance", within column D, directly enter the value 0 into cell D2, and then in cell D3 enter the formula =C3/C$8, and drag this down to fill to D7. This formula derives the percentage chance that the frequency represents, and this column is the actual representation of the probability that an item will drop from the roll table. You can try to change the values in the "Frequency" column and observe that the values in the "Percentage Chance" column automatically update.

Next, we will create the "Chance Value" in column A, that will eventually be used when a random roll is executed, to determine which item is awarded (Table 3.7). Enter 0 into cell A2 and underneath in cell A3 enter the formula =SUM(D$2:D2). Drag this down to fill the column to A7. This formula sums the values from the "Percentage Chance" column, progressively adding the values with each copy of

Table 3.7   Spreadsheet Mock-Up Showing the Formulas Needed for a Drop Table Simulation

	A	B	C	D
1	CHANCE VALUE	ITEM NAME	FREQUENCY	PERCENTAGE CHANCE
2	0	N/A	0	0
3	=SUM(D$2:D2)	Apple	100	=C3/C$8
4	=SUM(D$2:D3)	Banana	100	=C4/C$8
5		Pear	100	
6		Orange	100	
7		Mango	100	
8			=SUM(C2:C7)	

Note that on row 2 there are zero values along with the "N/A" entry. For the mechanics of this calculation to work as intended, these must be here. They do not interfere with the item drops generated.

Table 3.8 Spreadsheet Mock-Up Showing the Formula Needed to Calculate Random Drops

F	G
DROP NUMBER	DROPS
1	=VLOOKUP(RAND(),$A$2:$B$7,2,TRUE)
2	
3	
4	
5	
6	
7	
8	
9	
10	

the formula in the successive rows. This may initially seem counterintuitive. The reason for this summation is that we must take the values from the "Percentage Chance" column and put them into an order that will allow us to generate a random number and then compare it with these values in the "Chance Column" and derive the Item Dropped. This is shown below in Table 3.8.

To help keep the simulation looking clean and concise, leave a column gap and into cell F1 enter the name "Drop Number", then from F2 to F11 enter the numbers 1 to 10. This is simply numbering the drops. You can extend this down further and roll many times, which realistically, this is something that will be necessary for a full game project.

Enter the name "Drops" in cell G1 and then in cell G2 enter the formula = VLOOKUP(RAND(),$A$2:$B$7,2,TRUE).

This formula compares values across columns, returning desired results. The first parameter is the value that the function will look up, and in this case we are nesting the function RAND() within the VLOOKUP as the first parameter. The RAND() function generates a random number between 0 and 1. The second parameter can be thought of as a "sub-table" within the spreadsheet. In this case $A$2:$B$7 is essentially the same as A2 to A7, alongside B2 to B7. The third parameter specifies the column number to look up relative to the number of columns specified within the "sub-table" from parameter 2. For example, in this case, there are two columns, A and B, and A would be the number 1, B the number 2. The final parameter tells the function whether to look for an exact match or an approximate match. This must be set to TRUE for an approximate match in this case, as in a similar fashion to the experience points simulation, we are taking advantage of the default behavior of this function to allow our simulation to produce the desired results, that is, the function always reverts to the next smallest value if it does not find the value it is looking for. A word of caution. Taking advantage of default behaviors and, at times, brute forcing results can be a valid way of solving problems within spreadsheets. However, it is vital to make sure the simulation is well tested to be certain that there are no false results generated.

To summarize, in this case, the VLOOKUP takes the random number generated from the RAND() in the first parameter and looks for this value in the range A2 to A7. It will not find this value specifically, but will default to the next smallest value. The function will return the corresponding entry within the range B2 to B7. This produces the result of the random drop. Regenerate the random numbers several times and you will see the resulting drops changing. With all the values in the "Frequency" column set as the same, there will be an equal chance for any item to drop each time the random numbers are regenerated. You can try increasing one of the values within the frequencies column, which will give a higher drop chance to the corresponding item in the row, and if you continue to regenerate the random numbers you will see this item appearing more often in the "Drops" column.

This covers the basics of creating a random drop simulation within Excel. This method is a fairly robust and self-contained way to generate random rewards within a game. In general, this could become a section of a larger game economy simulation, considering that games drop various types of items for players. One example would be the ways in which this ties in to the monetization systems, such as calculating the behavior of a premium loot crate.

Pipeline and Getting Features into the Game

The term pipeline is one that you will come across frequently within the world of video game development. This term may have different meanings depending on the area of game development to which it is referring. As there are several different disciplines (and subdisciplines) all working together, one question that can arise is the notion of how everything constituting a game – code, art, design, systems, environments, characters, and many more – all come together into a coherent whole as a playable game experience. Essentially, this idea is covered by what we call the "pipeline", which is the process of going from the concept, through design, all the way to final completion of a game project. This covers aspects of detailed project management, and these can also be broken down into certain subsets, such as the art pipeline, referring to the methods by which the art team get their art assets into the game. The art must go from being created using specialized art software to being moved into the game engine to become integrated into the game that the player experiences. From the game economy designer's standpoint, our concern with the pipeline comes down to working with programmers and artists to move from hypothetical systems of gameplay loops described within a document and modeled with a spreadsheet, to something that essentially appears and is working for the player within the game. It is very difficult, in practice, to gain experience of this part of design without actually working on and shipping games, as it involves solving specific problems relative to projects and working with more technical disciplines that make the tangible artifacts of the game.

As the economy designer with a system that is planned out and modeled, the first port of call is to liaise with the programmer who is going to be implementing your system, and from here you need to communicate concisely how the system is designed to work in a practical sense, to allow this programmer to understand the design goals. This is where the design documentation will come into play, with programmers typically scrutinizing the document. A competent programmer should analyze your design and make sense of it from their own technical standpoint and come back to you with open questions related to how the implementation may affect the behavior of your design. This relationship between the designer and programmer working together to turn a design into a reality is one of the key creative elements of game design. It is a type of communication skill that can be difficult to quantify, but is an important part of being a professional game designer and working on a project.

Integrated into this process of working with a programmer, you will be required to think through and plan what controls you need for this system, and how they can be implemented by a programmer. The controls are often in the form of the values or variables you require in order to manipulate the system. These may be referred to as balancing values, changing the pacing, rate or intensity of certain systems.

It is probable that you will be using a bespoke tool, or web-based system, or possibly special customized aspects of the game engine in order to enter in the settings and/or controlling values. It is part of the programmer's role to implement this for the designer, essentially leaving "hooks" for the designer to come in and manipulate the values and other settings. This can become complicated, and economy designers often have to maintain a large number of settings and numerical values.

Coming back to the first example of a spreadsheet model, concerning a system of account leveling with experience points, how would this be entered into the game?

This will involve creating some variables in tandem with the programmer. In this case, the value of the player's experience points will need to be tracked, and this will mainly be handled by the programmer. There will be variables called "xp_points" or similar. These will hold the summed value of experience points the player gains from playing matches.

For the progression system to work, the player's experience points will need to be compared to experience points threshold values for each level. In essence, this will involve moving Table 3.2 into the backend software systems. One solution you can work on with programmers is to use a Comma Separate Values (CSV) file. A CSV is a special file that allows tabular data to be saved as plain text. The table can be entered as shown into a spreadsheet, and spreadsheet software typically allows the user to export the sheet to a CSV file. From here, bespoke functionality within the game's backend systems would allow this CSV to be uploaded. This is a simple example, and while a game designer does not need extensive programming knowledge, it is important to have an understanding of methods such as these and to be able to move from a theoretical design into a practical set of steps and settings that can be entered into the game's backend controlling software.

Balancing

With systems functional within the game, how do we go about knowing if the values entered, such as the amounts of currencies given, the experience points awarded and many others are such that they provide the most enjoyment to players? Are these values appropriate to keep the player's pace at a rate that is not too fast or slow, and for a free-to-play game, do these values help push players toward conversion? This process is known as balancing and is an extensive topic.

In general, there are three strategies for balancing the controlling values within a game economy. The first undertaking will be to use the spreadsheets you have created. You will run the simulations many times and analyze the results. Do the pacing of progression and the quantities of currencies and resources generated by the sources make sense? You should be able to get an idea of a meaningful starting point for balancing at this stage, and you will, for example, quickly see if your systems are going to generate far too much currency early on in the user's journey.

Working in combination with the spreadsheets, it is very important to get feedback from testers and, in tandem with this, to test out the systems yourself. Spreadsheets will only tell you so much, but testers will provide more information about the general feel of the game economy. Are the systems engaging beyond the raw values of resources players are getting? At this point, there will be opportunities for iteration, and any flaws in the design will surface.

Often, in game design circles we say that players blow our expectations out of the water the moment the game goes live. During live operations, it will be imperative to monitor telemetry data generated by the game in order to analyze the average behavior and performance of the player base. More information about maintaining a game's systems, along with analytics is covered in Chapter 5.

The Basics of Mathematics

As mentioned above, it can be very helpful for the economy designer to have a working knowledge of mathematics. As a math graduate, I have noticed that whenever the topic of mathematics arises, for a large number of people it will elicit something not too dissimilar from the gag reflex. It is curious how people acknowledge many of the skills encountered in life as simply requiring practice to improve, but treat mathematics differently. I have a suspicion that mathematics education systems have a tendency to foster this attitude. When learning new skills, there is some truth in people having a natural aptitude, but there is always the potential for growth. I believe that certain disciplines lend themselves to a wider spectrum of people being willing and able to engage with them. However, as far as math as an academic subject is concerned, the barrier to entry may be high, and the steep learning curve involved at the beginning can cause it to be less appealing as a learning process. Essentially, for many, the frustration phase at the beginning is just too strong to be overcome, unless we encounter the right teacher at the right time.

The good news is that mathematics is a subject that can be practiced and learned like any other, and it will be nothing but beneficial for the economy designer to become comfortable with the basics.

There are ways in which mathematics can be directly applied to game development, but in reality, this crops up only sporadically and often on an extremely ad hoc basis. For this section, therefore, rather than covering various theories, such as the types of progression curves (which can effectively be covered in more detail through other online resources), I think it might be beneficial to look at some of the basics of algebra and attempt to relate this to key game economy concepts such as progression system design and random number generation. This is intended to provide some degree of comfort with mathematics and provide a baseline from which you can further research the problems you are trying to solve.

Basic Algebraic Manipulation

To address the essential concepts that are involved in mathematics relevant to game development, I will cover the manipulation of terms. This will help not only in spreadsheets but also with other types of game systems design. This goes back to the very basics of early high school mathematics and will be trivially straightforward to some. For others, however, it will be important to cover the bases and begin to explore this fundamental knowledge and skill necessary for spreadsheets and any formulas used within the design of systems: experience points, health, damage, to name several.

First, consider the following: $3 + 2 = 5$. This is of course obvious at a glance, but what is important is not the result, but the fact that this is written out in a way that you can read from left to right. It is essentially a mathematical way of saying "Three plus two equals five". Now consider the following: $3 + x = 5$. For many, this instantly causes a slight panic. The moment we mix letters with numbers it is not something that we instantly recognize as familiar. The presence of the "x" is a mathematical way of saying that "three plus something equals five" and is by definition an equation because of the equals sign. Of course, two is the only possible number in this case, which is trivial, but the key is recognizing that the "x" is defined as a variable. This is a key foundation of mathematics, allowing us to express variable quantities within equations and to then manipulate these variables. It is also a basis for algebra. Collectively, the things making up an equation are called terms, be they variables or numbers, or other mathematical objects.

We can now take this a step further and go with one of the most important rules of manipulating terms within an equation: the "Change Side, Change Sign" rule. When you move any term to the opposite side of the equals sign, if it is positive, it becomes negative, and if it is negative, it becomes positive. If it is a multiplication, it becomes a division and vice versa.

With the above example, we can move the "3" from the left side of the equals sign to the right side of the equals sign. Therefore, this would become $x = 5 - 3$, which, consistent with the initial common sense observation, becomes $x = 2$. So we have essentially "solved this equation", by using algebraic manipulation to find the "unknown term" which is x in this case.

Within the context of game design, becoming comfortable with this basic concept of algebraic manipulation will serve you well for many parts of building game economies, for example, with regard to planning progression systems and the details of how experience points are distributed and calculated.

With this basic concept in mind, we can now "level up" with the idea of breaking the brackets – something that you will often see within mathematical expressions.

Breaking the Brackets

It is valuable to understand brackets in mathematical expressions, especially for some of the "under the surface" calculations which may arise as part of modeling game economies. One point to note here relates to context, and in relation to computers, there are many different conventions with notation specific to computer science. In this section, I am referring to the use of brackets within algebraic expressions, following specific rules. Within spreadsheet software, the algebraic rules of breaking brackets and manipulating terms can be applied, although one must also be aware of the different syntax required. The use of brackets for containing parameters to be entered into formulas is a different, bespoke case relevant to spreadsheet software.

Consider the mathematical expression $3(4 + 2)$. How would you evaluate this expression? The first thing to note with this method of notation is that the number 3 right next to the bracket signifies that this 3 must be multiplied with whatever is inside the bracket. The second rule is that everything within the bracket must be multiplied by whatever is outside the bracket. The most intuitive way to approach this is to add the 4 and the 2 to give 6, and then multiply this by the 3, giving the answer of 18.

However, there is another way you could think about this evaluation. If you were to multiply the 3 by the 4 to give 12 and then multiply the 3 by the 2 to give 6, then sum these results, $12 + 6$, to give 18, we arrive at the same result. This second way of thinking about evaluating brackets is the key to working with them.

Next, consider a similar expression, but this time with a variable: $3(x + 2)$. We cannot meaningfully add the number x to the number 2, so we must work with the alternate thought process as shown above. Multiply the 3 by the x to get 3x (a way of writing "3 multiplied by x"), and then multiply the 3 by the 2 to give 6. Therefore, the expression without the brackets is the same as writing $3x + 6$. This is as far as this expression can go in terms of evaluation. As it is, there is no way of knowing what x could be. However, this can be addressed by changing the expression into an equation.

Let's say we make up a new expression, one that is actually an equation: $3(x + 2) = 12$. For the left-hand side of the equals sign, we can evaluate this as above, $3x + 6 = 12$. Now we are in familiar territory, we move the 6 to the right-hand side to get $3x = 12 - 6$. Therefore, $3x = 6$, and as the rule of "Change Side, Change Sign" applies, when the 3 moves over to the right-hand side of the equals, it changes from multiplication to a division, so $x = 6/3$, which is 2.

This illustrates how one simple rule forms the foundation, and further rules build upon this. You may also find that you reverse engineer equations and expressions to introduce brackets, as these can begin to look more tidy, and will be necessary for more complex calculations.

This is the epitome of problem solving, where from a simple series of rules, we start to see overlap and can reapply different methods within different situations to derive solutions to problems.

With this knowledge in mind, brackets should become easier to manipulate and use within formulas, especially within spreadsheet calculations that are an essential part of game economy design.

A Practical Example

Becoming comfortable with the foundations of algebra will be of significant benefit for game economy design. Even if used indirectly, this knowledge and understanding will surface during the development of many metagame-related features. The following details an example of applying knowledge from mathematics to progression system design.

Consider a game where you must define the number of experience points required to reach each account level. A starting point can be to use the triangular numbers as the basis. The triangular numbers is a sequence as follows:

$$1, 3, 6, 10, 15, 21, \ldots$$

They are derived via the following pattern. The first triangular number is 1. The second adds 2 to the 1, giving 3. The third adds 3 to the previous triangular number, giving 6. The fourth adds 4 to the previous triangular number, giving 10, and so on. This can be shown via Table 3.9.

Table 3.9   The First Six Triangular Numbers and the Method Used to Calculate Them

Index (n)	1	2	3	4	5	6
Method		+2	+3	+4	+5	+6
Triangular Number	1	3	6	10	15	21

We can think of the Index as the count of numbers. For example, the 4th triangular number is 10.

There is a formula to find the nth triangular number:

$$T(n) = 0.5n(n+1)$$

We can therefore find, for example, the 12th triangular number, by plugging the value 12 into the formula in place of the n, as follows:

$$T(12) = 0.5 * 12(12+1) = 78$$

To apply this concept to experience points within a progression system, we can use the triangular numbers to define how many experience points are needed for the player to reach each account level. However, it would be prudent to increase the range of these values. We can simply multiply the formula by 100 to achieve this, becoming:

$$\text{Xp Required to Reach Level } n = 50n(n+1)$$

Table 3.10 shows the experience points the player requires to reach each level, which is a table that you will include with your spreadsheets and documentation.

This will be expanded further, and you can calculate the requirements for any level quickly. For example, to reach level 10, the player would have to attain $50 * 10(10 + 1) = 5500$ Xp.

As a relation to algebraic manipulation, we can multiply the 50n outside the brackets by everything inside the brackets, giving $50n^2 + 50n$. However, this would be cleaner if it was written as $50(n^2 + n)$, reversing this process to add the brackets back in. You may see this same formula written in this form, so if you are researching, it becomes important to recognize this.

Table 3.10   Table Showing the Experience Points Required to Reach Each Player Level

PLAYER LEVEL (N)	XP REQUIRED
1	100
2	300
3	600
4	1000
5	1500
6	2100
And so on...	

As a final point, consider the following:

During the development of this system, we may be interested in carrying out some analysis and can reverse engineer this. For the sake of argument, if we know the amount of experience points a player has attained, can we deduce the level they have reached by way of the formula?

For example, if the player has attained 5500 Xp as above, but we are looking to find what level the player has reached, the formula would become:

$$5500 = 50n(n+1)$$

We can move the 50 from right to left, therefore dividing the 5500 by 50, giving:

$$110 = n(n+1)$$

How would we solve this equation to find n? This is where some further knowledge of mathematics is required. For reference, we can multiply out the brackets and re-arrange this to become $n^2 + n - 110 = 0$. This is a *quadratic equation* and can be solved using the quadratic formula. There are many resources online that can be used here if you are unfamiliar with this discipline. There are also plenty of websites which will automatically solve quadratic equations.

This particular quadratic equation has two solutions, $n = 10$ and $n = -11$. The reason for the two solutions is due to the quadratic formula. This may seem counterintuitive, but mathematically both solutions exist. However, this is where mathematical systems and their practical application to game design deviate. Of course, the negative solution is not relevant in this case and can be disregarded.

The Coupon Collector Problem

The Coupon Collector problem relates to the field of probability and is one of many fascinating areas of mathematics. Probability as a discipline within mathematics reaches a level of complexity far beyond that required for pragmatic game economy design. However, we can boil this down to something intelligible that can be applied within game design.

The coupon collector problem is as follows:

Consider a contest that involves collecting N unique coupons from cereal boxes. Every cereal box contains one unique coupon, with every coupon having the same chance of being present in a cereal box. How many boxes do you need to open in order to collect at least one coupon of each type?

On the surface, this seemingly simple question has a complex solution, which runs deep into the theory of probability. But it should also be obvious that this problem can have some relevance in terms of game development, particularly when it comes to the design of random rewards, and by extension, other related systems involving the idea of random number generation to provide content.

To return to the original question, it can be phrased in a different way: If there are N different coupons, each having the same probability to be drawn and coupons can be replaced after a draw, how many draws do you expect to have to make before you have collected each of the N coupons at least once?

The answer to this question is always going to be an approximation, but this can be calculated with a formula:

$$\text{Approximate number of draws needed} = N * Ln(N) + N * \gamma + 0.5$$

The formula comes with the following notes:

- N is the total number of different coupons to be collected.
- γ is a mathematical constant called the Euler-Mascheroni constant, which can be approximated to 0.57721.
- The logarithm (identified by the "Ln") is the natural logarithm, meaning that it is a logarithm to the base e, where e is Euler's Number; another mathematical constant which is approximately equal to 2.71828. The logarithm is defined as the inverse to exponentiation and has a wide range of applications within mathematics, engineering and many other fields of study. You can find the natural logarithm formula within calculator and spreadsheet programs and use this without the need of a deep mathematical understanding of the concept.

An example of this formula in use would be as follows:

There are 60 coupons. What is the estimated number of draws that someone would need to take in order to draw all 60 coupons at least once?

The approximate number of draws is $60*Ln(60) + 60*0.57721 + 0.5 = 280.7933$, so we can say that the approximate number of draws is 281 to collect all 60 coupons.

This concept instantly throws up a parallel with the idea of a loot box within video games: a system whereby players interact with some type of object that dispenses a random reward, and duplicates of the reward are possible. This is connected to the idea of replacement considered within the coupon collector problem. This can then be expanded to cover any system where a random drop is a key part of the design.

As part of your thought process while planning a system requiring random drops, you will be required to gauge how much content players will gain. This will tie into other aspects such as the number and length of play sessions for the average player, as well as for the extremely committed player. If there is specific content tied to the random drops, this will need to be built by other departments within the company, such as 3D modelers. As part of this process, using this formula will give you an idea of what players need to do to gain all of your planned content, and this is invaluable information. One major proviso is that this is just a measure and only applies directly if the chance for each drop is equal. In practice, within the design of loot boxes and gacha, the chance of each drop being equal is very rarely the case, but nevertheless as an approximation and a starting point, applying this formula is a quick way to set a design on its course, concerning the time and money required to build content and its supporting distribution systems.

References

Game Balance (first edition), Ian Schreiber & Brenda Romero, 2022

Game Design: Theory and Practice (second edition), Richard Rouse III, 2005

Game Wisdom: Theories on Game Design, "Debating Difficulty Curves in Game Design", 2021. https://game-wisdom.com/critical/debating-difficulty-game-design

Gameplay and Design, Kevin Oxland, 2004

Make Use Of, "11 Ways Progression Works in Video Games", 2022. https://www.makeuseof.com/video-game-progression-ways

PositivePsychology.com, "What Iis the Peak-End Rule? How to Use Iit Smartly", 2019. https://positivepsychology.com/what-is-peak-end-theory

Thinking, Fast and Slow, Daniel Kahneman, 2011

4
MONETIZATION

Monetization within video games can be a sensitive topic within player and developer communities. It must be stressed that if the entire games industry can be considered as rapidly evolving, then monetization within the games industry is even more swiftly evolving. The practices that are accepted during a period of two to three years will inevitably change, and developers must stay ahead of the curve, monitoring the current trends to keep their approach to development accepted by the target audience for their project.

During the early days of the video games industry, monetization design was characterized as the basic design of the game in relation to the business model. Consider an arcade game such as *Space Invaders* which now has a well-recognized standard design practice of giving the player three lives for each play session. The player puts money into the machine, can play until they fail three times, and then is required to put more money in the machine. This simple concept is essentially the precursor to more intricate session control systems which are observed in modern free-to-play titles.

The shift from arcades to home computer systems and consoles brought about the distribution of games via retail purchase on physical media such as ROM cartridges and floppy disks. This resulted in a change in the way video games were consumed, with video games introduced into the comfort of the home. A higher initial cost for both hardware and software provided the freedom for players to engage in and switch between multiple titles. Then e-commerce happened with digital distribution and digital goods. This led to microtransactions, downloadable content (DLC), free-to-play, advertising and made monetization a distinct topic in itself. More subtle developments in design trends then came about, shifting the developers from coercive strategies, such as the "pay to win" approach, and moved onto providing a better premium experience for players.

DOI: 10.1201/9781003386865-5

In the context of a practical working life, monetization is often encompassed within the parent term: game economy. How this is framed within the practical realities of working life can be varied. In fact, in my own career, I have worked as a Monetization Designer and a Game Economy Designer, and the day-to-day tasks and responsibilities were the same. This chapter will explore some of those tasks and responsibilities.

Design around the Core Business Models

There are different ways of breaking down current video game business models, but if we look at the highest level, we can see two distinct routes: a product that is free at the point of entry and a premium product that requires an upfront cost. Naturally, whether the product is free-to-play or premium has a significant influence on the overall design direction and the experience the developers intend to create for players. Defined early in the process, this overall goal must be adhered to when making the multiple design decisions that surface during development. However, in terms of the pragmatic process of building a game, which takes the form of a series of problems to be solved with the development resources at hand, one can compartmentalize aspects of monetization into a set of relatively discrete (with natural overlap) methods, strategies and best practices that can be employed within games. Some of these strategies can be combined with a natural synergy, and some are much more commonly observed within free-to-play titles than others.

You can think of the design elements discussed within this chapter as a designer's toolkit, pertaining to overall strategies for monetization, along with some of the finer elements which can be readily applied to your strategy.

Monetization Strategies: Performance, Preference and Personalization

With the core business models – free-to-play and premium product – in mind, we begin to think about different monetization strategies. These can be broken down into three overarching strategies that different games use: The *performance strategy*, the *preference strategy* and the *personalization strategy*.

From a holistic viewpoint, these strategies are guidelines for the game's design to follow, and there is some overlap along the often blurred lines between the strategies. Some methods will lend themselves more to free-to-play titles than others. There are edge cases and discrete topics which cannot be accurately categorized. As always with the games industry, innovations happen regularly.

The *performance strategy* aims to monetize the power of players, with the player spending money to acquire objects, elements or aspects that increase the effectiveness of content available, or accelerate access to more powerful content. This strategy is the most aggressive in terms of the direct effect of monetization on the core gameplay. Commonly used with free-to-play mobile games, this often involves the entire progression and game economy built around the monetization. In its purest form, the performance strategy would become the controversial pay-to-win methodology, but there exists debate with many modern game design approaches as to whether they in fact genuinely constitute paying to win. During the earlier days of the mobile games industry, a blatant pay-to-win design was more accepted, but has in subsequent years generated a large amount of vitriol among gamers.

The *preference strategy* aims to widen the base of playstyles and versatility of the gameplay by way of monetization. In many instances this does have ties with the performance strategy, but while there is overlap, the preference strategy aims to be more creative in its attempts to avoid outright power monetization. Typically, these games attempt to use real-world spending to accelerate the unlock of a preferred playstyle. For example, purchasing a premium weapon blueprint within *Call of Duty: Modern Warfare II* gives the player a predefined variant of a base weapon within the game, but with modifications pre-equipped on this weapon blueprint. The player can attain the exact same configurations by playing with the base weapon and unlocking all modifications to this weapon, but by purchasing the blueprint weapon the player gets a pre-configured weapon to enjoy. In some sense, the player is buying around the need to play with a weapon to level it up, but they never receive anything that gives them an absolute power advantage. The free ways to play may require more play time, but they always ultimately give the player the same potential power as if they had paid.

The *personalization strategy* aims to monetize the individual expression of the player, both on a personal level, but extending into the social aspects of games. This strategy involves purely selling cosmetic vanity items, which have no effect on the gameplay. An important, but also difficult problem for designers is the fact that when a game only sells cosmetic items for real-world currency (either directly or indirectly via a hard currency), this requires an extensive amount of art content to be produced (within Fortnite, for example) which becomes very expensive. More and more content must be produced during the game's lifespan, and this content must not only increase in quality and visual appeal, but the game itself must have a foundation for the creative bandwidth which will allow such content to be made. For example, there is more creative potential for various different types of cosmetic items within Fortnite than there would be within a game with a theme more grounded in reality. This is not to say that it is impossible, but creative limitations within a project's core theme and vision are very real issues developers face.

In reality, many games will involve a mixture of the three strategies defined above, and one could argue that many games strive to get to the preference strategy with many of their systems, especially when they involve competitive multiplayer as their core driving force. This begs the question of why a game of this nature should not simply avoid any risk of rousing anger among their player bases and go for the personalization strategy. First and foremost, creating cosmetic content is by far the most expensive way to monetize, and content treadmills involve players demanding better and better content the longer this goes on. However, we must remember that with monetization, we are looking to create positive real money gameplay experiences for players. You get a better game when you spend, as the holy grail of monetization, so games can legitimately include gameplay affecting aspects costing real money as a true part of their design vision, beyond the simple base requirement for games to monetize well to be financially viable.

Components of Monetization

The following details the aspects of video game monetization that are observed in many modern video games, covering the different genres, business models and monetization strategies.

Microtransactions (Hard Currency)

The use of micro-transactions within video games has become wide-spread with the rise in popularity of the free-to-play business model. Microtransactions allow players to spend real money from within a game, to obtain game-specific content such as virtual goods and virtual currencies.

The key strategy which is employed readily across the games industry is to introduce a special in-game currency, referred to as hard currency, for which the main method of acquiring is through micro-transactions. This centralizes the microtransactions within the game to a specific area of the front end and to a set series of purchases. Overall, the use of a hard currency opens the door to many further monetization strategies and will make the life of the designer far easier.

First, the value of the hard currency in relation to real-world currency tends to become obfuscated during a player's life cycle with a game. The hard currency should relate to the value of real-world currency, to the point where it can be noticed during purchase. For example, typically $1 = 100 hard currency is used as a basis for pricing, though other starting points may be favorable. From here, larger packs of hard currency can be sold, giving bonus amounts for larger real money purchases. As the player continues to engage with the game, small amounts of hard currency can be awarded through gameplay, along with repeated purchases and spending of hard currency. When combined with sales and promotions, this can somewhat distort the perception of value of hard currency. Using hard currency as the intermediary step disassociates the value of a virtual good with a real money value. This is where potential controversy can arise, and as games evolve, more honest and noticeable pricing is preferred by players.

While designers should proceed with caution with hard currency usage and pricing, there are further benefits. As mentioned, the ability to give away this currency in small amounts allows for certain otherwise paid rewards to be given to players who, for example, engage extensively with the game.

Using a hard currency provides flexibility and makes it far easier for a designer to pivot and adjust a design during a development cycle.

With backend controls concerned only with the hard currency, it can be applied easily to the different game content. Divorcing the technical aspects of integrating real money transactions with the monetization tasks of content planning, costing and selling of goods makes the designer far less dependent on other departments, a positive overall.

Consumable Items

Consumable items are items within games that are used by the player to produce some type of temporary effect, with the item being removed from the player's inventory once used. The consumable items serve as a means to give certain temporary benefits to players and can be a simple and powerful way to introduce monetization into a game. Consumables are ideal for driving repeat purchases, due to the temporary nature of the effects they provide. From a general design sense, they are useful to support even in conceptual form. If, for example, you want to provide players with multiple boosters that have some type of effect, but also want to allow the players to activate these boosters at their own discretion, then providing these rewards as consumable items is a solution to this problem.

Durable Items

Durable items are the opposite to consumable items. They are persistent and remain in the player's inventory once they are acquired. You can think of a durable item as a *property* of an item, rather than a *type* of item within a game. Durables will form the bulk of the premium cosmetic items within a game. If you have spent real-world money to acquire a vanity item, you will retain ownership of this item in your account permanently. The line between consumables and durables can seem to become blurred for certain loot driven games, where weapons and armor can be collected and sold to non-player character merchants. In general, these would still behave as durables, as their core purpose is not to be consumed. This contrasts with an item such as a health potion, whereby its only application within the game causes it to be used up.

Advertising

Integrating advertising into a video game as a form of monetization is a strategy that concerns mobile, free-to-play games. There are software systems that exist for integrating adverts into mobile games, and there are different types of adverts. This section covers the rewarded adverts from a design standpoint. I do not feel it is appropriate to cover the intricacies of how these systems pay out, as this is specific to different providers and can readily change over time. For the economy designer, the challenge is to find the best ways to integrate adverts into the game's design.

Banner Adverts

Banner adverts are adverts that are persistently displayed within an application. They typically occupy a small section of the screen and can be images or text. As with all monetization, it should be built from the ground up within the project. Banner adverts are passive, and certain genres of mobile games lend themselves to banner adverts more than others. If the game is a strategy or puzzle game, which involves the user staying within a single main screen while interacting with different elements on that screen, then banner adverts can be effective to implement. Working with a user interface artist, space within the screen can be built into the main game screen to show the banner advert without interfering with the game.

Interstitial Adverts   Interstitial adverts, when they appear in the game, take over the whole screen. Interstitial adverts can be of varying formats, ranging from static images, to animated GIFs, videos and interactive playable adverts. Once the advert displays on the screen, the players can close the advert, watch the video through the end, or they can tap on the advert and visit the destination page. The designer must consider the flow of the game when considering using interstitial adverts. Since they take over the screen they are more prominent, which is both a positive and a negative factor. Used in a poorly thought-out fashion, these will quickly become intrusive and disrupt the player's engagement. Interstitial adverts are best integrated into games that have natural transitions points, a trait that is found in many different types of games. Simply dividing a game into levels, for example in the fashion of a platform game, gives ample opportunity to use interstitial adverts between the levels.

Rewarded Video Adverts   Rewarded video adverts are an interesting way to tie advert monetization directly into your game economy. A rewarded video advert is an opt-in strategy, whereby the player is presented with the chance to watch an advert. When the player reaches a certain point in the game, they will be presented with the option to watch a short video advert, in return for receiving an in-game reward such as an amount of in-game currency, a power up or some other item; this is up to the designer. Rewarded video adverts are typically used alongside microtransactions as part of the overall monetization strategy. Naturally the barrier to the player opting in to watch a rewarded video is significantly less than spending real money through microtransactions, so in this case the rewarded video adverts would be used to complement real money spending, giving lesser rewards, but used in specific ways integrated into the gameplay and metagame. Conversely, the rewarded video adverts would not want to risk superseding the microtransactions, so careful consideration is required before deciding on their use.

The methods in which rewarded videos are integrated into games are built into the monetization design from the ground up. If the game has a hard currency which is mainly acquired through real money transactions, a starting point could be to give the user a small amount for watching a rewarded video, which would be limited in terms of how frequently this is available. However, it is common for developers to be a little more creative and integrate the opportunities for players to watch adverts in more intricate ways. Hyper-casual games which are extremely quick to pick up and play and center around simple arcade-like core mechanics can use rewarded adverts (and all types of adverts) effectively. Adverts could be used to give the player the opportunity to retry from a specific checkpoint if they fail, or used to provide a multiplier to the rewards for the level, potentially doubling the soft currency earned. These are just some of the common practices used when integrating rewarded video adverts into a mobile title. If you find yourself working on a project of this type, I would encourage plenty of initial research and then building a solid foundation to support small currency rewards, consumables or other cheap resources which can be given readily and often through rewarded adverts.

Battle Pass

The Battle Pass is a monetization system in which a series of rewards are presented to the player along a progression track. The progression track typically includes a set number of tiers. Each tier contains a reward, often one or more cosmetic items, or in-game resources such as hard currency. Progress through the tiers is typically controlled by bespoke experience points which the player earns by playing the game. The player can, at any point, carry out a real money transaction (either directly or via hard currency, often amounting to about $10), which allows the player to claim the rewards on all tiers they have reached. Certain tiers are designated as Free, providing their reward to the player upon simply reaching the tier without the need for the real money transaction. After a player carries out the initial purchase, some Battle Passes allow the player to carry out smaller subsequent transactions where they buy individual tiers.

A Battle Pass stays active for a finite amount of time, referred to as a season (60 days for example), after which point the cosmetic content is replaced, and player progress is reset (Figure 4.1).

The Battle Pass is centered around monetization, but also acts as a retention and engagement system. It applies time pressure on the player over months as opposed to minutes, and therefore the content on a Battle Pass derives its value from the time the player invests in the game. An item placed at the later tiers on the Battle Pass is inherently more valuable as it takes more time to reach. The methods for distributing the experience points that are required to progress through the tiers are often tied more to time invested rather than skill, although this depends on the design vision and type of game.

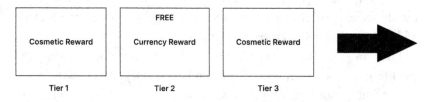

Figure 4.1 A basic mock-up of a Battle Pass design.

The Battle Pass is relatively aggressive in nature, but is widely accepted. For players who play the game but do not carry out the initial purchase, they will progress through the Battle Pass but be unable to claim the majority of content they unlock on tiers reached. For players invested in the game, this tends to create the feeling that they are wasting time by progressing without being able to claim their rewards, subtly coaxing them to convert and be instantly able to claim a plethora of cosmetic content. For players who do pay, they are instantly subjected to the time pressure of progressing the Battle Pass to get their money's worth in terms of rewards before the season expires, providing a powerful retention driver.

The distribution of rewards bleeds from one season into the next, and a notable use of a game's hard currency can potentially be observed by reaching the final tier of a Battle Pass. Sufficient hard currency is potentially provided via tier rewards to allow the player to purchase the Battle Pass for the subsequent season, again creating longer-term retention.

The emotions created with these systems are up for grabs by developers, and innovations in Battle Pass design such as the less linear approach seen in *Call of Duty: Modern Warfare II* have given players more control over the rewards which they can attain. While Battle Pass design varies slightly among different games, the key principles remain consistent.

Downloadable Content (DLC)

DLC refers to the practice of selling additional content for a video game which has already been released. DLC is typically used as a form of monetization, with the content being charged for, although at times developers will release free DLC as part of their postlaunch strategy.

The DLC content can take many forms, though you will commonly see expansions to a game's main campaign, which can include additional missions or story chapters.

DLC has become an established method for developers to expand the lifespan of a game, typically a standalone story driven experience.

A point to note regarding DLC is that the term is used to refer to additionally purchased content sold to players through the platform stores (e.g. Steam). Content which is purchased from within the game, through an in-game store, using hard currency would not be considered DLC in this sense. For information about in-game store, see the section titled "Premium In-Game Stores".

Subscriptions

Subscriptions are a popular method of paying for many online services, and with the growing popularity of Games-as-a-Service (GaaS), subscriptions can be effectively integrated into the monetization strategy.

Subscriptions within GaaS require special auto-renewing in-game purchases, which offer the user a series of benefits while the subscription is active. Like all monetization methods, this is most effective when creatively built into the game's design from the ground up. One noteworthy example is the *Fortnite Crew* subscription with the immensely popular *Fortnite*. This offers players a number of different benefits, including new cosmetic content and an amount of the game's premium currency each month. Therefore, the player gains items to own but also the choice of other items to purchase. To complement this, there are motivators for the player to keep the subscription active. First, the player gains access to the Battle Pass, and second there are legacy styles; unlockable variations of the monthly cosmetic content, which become successively available the longer the player remains subscribed.

Subscriptions are very much in line with contemporary developments within video game monetization, where games seek to give paying players a more enjoyable game, rather than a means to bypass playing. There must be an appropriate value proposition to players, which ties into the benefits that are given. What you are selling to players here is a benefit for a long-term commitment to the game.

Lootboxes

While the previous chapter covered the concept of gacha in the high-level sense that it encompasses the idea of randomness within a game economy, a more direct application of gacha mechanics is through lootboxes.

Lootboxes are items which are purchased (usually indirectly via a hard currency) for real money and are then opened (consumed), giving the player a randomly generated item. There are different methods for designing lootboxes as monetization within a game. Some free-to-play games tie lootboxes into their main system for progression, such as via upgrade of content. Players in this case will open lootboxes to gain resources used to upgrade the game's more prominent content such as cards within a collectible card game. In this case, players are nudged toward opening many lootboxes with the cap for spending typically running into the tens of thousands of dollars. This can be designed in an honest fashion as part of the free-to-play business model when it acts as a complement to a main gameplay loop, but is nevertheless designed to drive the player to repeatedly spend real money for small, random incremental rewards.

Lootboxes can also be used to award the player with cosmetic items, or potentially key content depending on the game (such as new characters in a hero collection game), and there are further nuances to the design of the gacha mechanic that designers can utilize. There are systems for gacha demanding that players repeatedly open lootboxes in order to collect a set of items, and in a general sense, by the very nature of a monetized gacha system, you are asking players to pay real money to take a chance at getting a reward. Legal complications regarding lootboxes have become a hotly debated topic and is something that the designer should research and keep up to date with. In various countries, they are now regulated under gambling laws, and there are constraints on the design, such as designers being forced to show the drop chances of the content within the lootbox to players. A rare reward would typically have an extremely small chance of dropping, and with this information becoming player-facing, some potential coercion becomes exposed.

In summary, the idea that the game should be fair to players persists throughout the concept of monetization. An analogy can be made with other aspects of game design, whereby a game that is punishing to players, via unexpected demands or rule changes, will not be as well received as a game which is difficult but nevertheless a true test of the player's skill: one that has a consistent ruleset which allows for depth of strategy and varied playstyles. In a similar fashion, this idea of fairness can be demonstrated through appropriate monetization design. Naturally, the non-paying players should be able to compete with payers as a base line, otherwise the game becomes a pay-to-win experience. Conversely, the players who have paid must have a place in the game and feel challenged. A fair playing field is what you are looking for.

Player Habits and Monetization Methods for Free-to-Play Games

Naturally, players will only monetize if they are going to keep coming back to a game. Having solid retention is a key aspect. However, there is another related, but ultimately separate key performance indicator metric called "stickiness" which is to be considered. This metric is covered in more detail in Chapter 5 and relates to how valuable a player perceives a game to be.

In terms of stickiness (or the "sticky factor") from a game economy design mindset, we can look for patterns in how players engage with the game's systems, considering the rewards they get, and how they use these. Going a little deeper, what we are looking for is a set of actions on many different levels, together with their associated emotions, that the player feels motivated to repeat. The goal is that the player will form a habit of playing the game to experience these emotions time and again. While the sticky factor is the goal, it can be extremely difficult to predict this. Essentially it requires trial and error while building systems, to find something that works. This is where the idea of game economy theory and the practical side of simply building, testing and iterating based on flow and feel diverge from one another. There are retention systems, features and various design elements that can be used to induce the sticky factor, but there is no magic formula to this. A feature alone will not cause miraculous stickiness, but when these, combined with everything else in the game, all go into the mix, they can create positive effects on the habits of players.

With stickiness playing its part and players coming back and seeing value in the game, you will increase the chances for players to pass through the barrier to an initial spend, thus fulfilling your goal of monetization. If we achieve a strong game economy and a monetization design that builds the entire strategy into the DNA of the game, let us go on to consider some of the best indirect design practices forming the key to free-to-play monetization design.

Pinch Points

The concept of a pinch point is critical within free-to-play design. A pinch point occurs after a certain amount of time has been spent playing a game, where the player runs out of something valuable, creating a soft block on progress. This includes but is not limited to an in-game currency. When implemented effectively, the player is pushed toward spending real-world money to overcome the pinch point. At this time, it becomes essential to address the reality that only a small percentage of players will ever monetize to bypass the pinch point (spending for the first time is referred to as "conversion"). The game must provide methods for non-paying players to progress beyond the pinch point. These will typically involve some degree of grinding or waiting for timers to expire.

A common example of a pinch point would be a game where the player has a number of lives. The pinch point can be created with the player running out of lives at a certain point when faced with a series of difficult levels. The player would then be nudged into carrying out a microtransaction to acquire extra lives.

Pinch points are relative to the genre of game you are creating, and the concept can run deeper, utilizing the in-game currencies and resources that are often prevalent within free-to-play games. Because pinch points are typically noticeable to players, it is a good practice to keep them honest within the context of the game. The fact that a player loses lives for dying within a game is an accepted convention, although the concept of a punishing gameplay mechanic is not. Similarly, spending a currency regularly is accepted as part of the core loop. The pinch point can be created with the player eventually running out of in-game money with the currency sinks increasing in magnitude, ahead of the rate at which player earns this currency.

To dive a little deeper into the complexities of creating pinch points within a game, consider a game where there are in-game currencies working in tandem with other specific resources. For example, within the game *Marvel Snap*, the core loop of progression involves upgrading cards using a soft currency called Credits, along with card-specific resources called Boosters. In this case, the pinch point can be created with the idea that the Credits will be used up faster than Boosters.

This concept of having multiple resources, with one designed to run out via a source which does not keep up with its associated sinks, is a relatively common practice within titles which involve multiple specific resources and avenues to progress. This makes the balancing task easier for designers as they maintain a high level of control over progression (typically in the form of upgrading content) with the specific resource, while introducing a pinch point with the main soft currency.

To design the timing and gameplay required to reach a pinch point requires extensive spreadsheet modeling of the game economy. With the basic techniques covered in the previous chapter, this sets the stage for more complex calculations concerning earning and spending of in-game currencies. From here the designer will know the time in game and/or number of sessions an average player will take to reach the point where their in-game currency sources cannot keep up with sinks, therefore producing the pinch point.

After a user has converted, they are far more likely to spend repeatedly; the initial barrier to spending has been removed. For players who spend to overcome the pinch point, they can be tracked as "spenders", and it is now up to the creativity of the designer to find ways in which to coax players into spending more.

Energy Systems

Energy systems, on the surface, can seem like an aggressive way of outright limitation on the player's ability to play a game. An energy system uses some type of specific resource, often an in-lore equivalent of the eponymous "energy", which depletes each time the player enters into the main gameplay (be it a mission, match, round, etc.). Over time the energy refills, allowing for more play, and the player can often choose to spend an amount of hard currency to refill their energy.

For the designer, what reasons are there to use such an obvious tactic?

The primary reason for using the energy system is session control, designed to eventually instill a habit in players. Energy systems put strong control of player engagement into the hands of the designers. The amount of energy that is available for a single play session determines the length of that play session. By extension the rate at which the energy refills helps to guide the frequency of play sessions. The culminating effect of this will, ideally, be that these play sessions become integrated into the player's daily routine. The end goal here is to have a positive effect on retention, which is a key metric for effective monetization of free-to-play titles.

Without the energy system, players would have more means to binge on the game and potentially burn through content. This is another important reason for using an energy system: the pacing of content. During live operations, if players are consuming content faster than the team can produce it, this will lead to problems and players will lose interest in the game. The energy system is another theoretical way for designers to apply the brakes on player progress and engagement if it is getting out of control.

Direct monetization is incorporated into energy systems, but would rarely be seen as a core reason to introduce an energy system itself. It is often seen as a somewhat crude way to charge players real-world money. Nevertheless, the overarching concept of paying to bypass a waiting time certainly comes into play. There is a slight contradiction here in that the main purpose of the energy system is to control the player's engagement and content consumption, but paying real money opens up the possibility of breaking the energy system's intent. Of course, developers naturally welcome players spending their money on the game, but the overall design must allow those players who spend money to have a good premium experience with the game.

The aggressive use of the energy system is an area that is interestingly open to some innovation from designers. Are there ways in which we can achieve a similar effect, but disguised in some way? The game *Clash Royale* awards the player with chests for winning matches, of which the player can only store a set amount, and each chest has an active timer delaying its opening. This design does not directly restrict the player from playing the game, but if they do continue to play, they cannot store their rewards and will lose them. They can either wait for a chest to open or pay to bypass a timer. This is just one example of an energy system cleverly built into a game in a modified fashion. We can extrapolate other methods from this with some games building different devices into their gameplay loops, in order to achieve similar goals.

Loss Aversion (Reward Removal)

There is a cognitive bias known as the Negativity Bias, which determines that negative events tend to have a more significant impact on our psychological state than positive events. This is a bias which is related to the idea of loss aversion, that is, players will typically feel a more powerful emotional connection to a loss of a particular magnitude, compared to a gain of equal magnitude. Within game design, this effect can be used to drive monetization in a potentially powerful way. As a hypothetical example, within an RPG game, the difficulty curve can be controlled to allow players to progress, gaining rewards through the game's quests by dedicating just enough effort so that they remain invested. This would lead all the way up to an important boss battle. The difficulty of the fight would then subtly spike causing the player to be defeated and lose all their rewards. However, the game would include a special Reincarnation consumable potion, which would bring the player character back to life, reinstating their rewards. This potion would mainly be available through microtransactions and could be offered to the player directly upon defeat by the boss. Alternatively, the process could be drawn out, disguising the ways that the player is pushed into acquiring and using this potion. Regardless of the process, the negativity bias increases the impact of losing gained rewards after defeat, and this is more likely to cause players to (eventually) spend real-world money, simply to avoid this.

Cosmetic Items

Cosmetic items are items which have absolutely no effect on the gameplay and are used by players to show off a visual style to other players, allowing for a type of social comparison within multiplayer games. Cosmetic items can also be used for the benefit of the player themselves, to allow them to create and see their own identity within the game.

Vanity items complement free cosmetics (if you have any), as the player will assign a value to non-premium content in relation to premium content.

Regarding cosmetic items, one vital factor that designers must take into account is that pure cosmetic items require time and money to produce. Once the item is produced it enters the store and is sold.

Players who buy it will own and enjoy it for a while, but ultimately will seek new things to buy; it won't satisfy as a single item forever. Developers will need to keep adding new and interesting cosmetics, in order to appeal to different tastes. However, items don't have any true obsolescence within the game. This is an interesting aspect of digital items; they don't wear out in the same way as real-world items do. Players who pay for cosmetics therefore end up in situations where they accrue many items and still the developers need to add new ones to maintain player satisfaction. This is a good example of a content treadmill (See Chapter 5). To some extent there is no way around this when you are monetizing a game with cosmetic items, but be aware that this method does involve developers throwing money at a problem.

A key design approach for cosmetic items is to realize that there is really no magic or mathematical way of modeling whatever is going to appeal to different players. The only way to know what will work is to go out and ask your audience. Working with the community team within a game development company is where you will gain insight into this. You will also look at sales data which will quickly tell you what sells and what does not. Certain patterns will emerge. From my own experience, I have noticed that items that looked like real-world superhero characters or items within a customization system that allowed players to build characters resembling popular heroes or villains tended to sell well.

This does not mean that the designer must be completely oblivious to the content being made. Even with different items appealing to different tastes, it is still essential for the designers on any project to create guidelines for content (see rarity guide) which will help the artists to create distinguishing features on various items. This is important in demonstrating varying levels of content. Each game needs to have its equivalent of the Ferrari, otherwise known as Veblen goods.

The following lists are designed to provide some creative inspiration for the types of items you may consider.

Character Skins

These are changes to the visual appearance of player characters within the game. They can include full outfits that the character wears and may include various different items of clothing and armor. As an example, the character customization seen in contemporary fighting games such as the later entries within the *Tekken* series allows for extensive changes to the visual appearance of the character's apparel.

Weapon Skins

Similar to character skins, weapon skins are unique visual appearances for weapons within a game. Typically these relate to decals and patterns that players can apply to firearms within games involving gun combat.

Vehicle Skins

Games involving vehicles can allow players to change the visual appearance of these vehicles. Similar to character customization, vehicle customization can become complex.

Emotes and Animations

Emotes are character animations that the player can trigger during gameplay. They are often used to represent certain emotions from the player during multiplayer games. Examples include a hand wave or a brief dance. There can also be other animations or gestures that can be introduced into the game, such as specific death animations.

Loading Screens

A type of cheaper cosmetic content could take the form of specifically designed loading screens, including possible promotional artwork.

Emblems and Banners

Within a game's front end, there will often be a representation of the gamer's handle or username shown in some area of the screen. On matchmaking screens this is also very likely to appear. There is the opportunity to add personalization around this, with small emblem images, and/or banner images surrounding the player's name. These are typically very cheap cosmetics to produce, and games tend to use these extensively as small rewards for gameplay challenges or similar. They may be useful to include as inexpensive content that is part of a larger bundle, centering around a specific theme.

Pets and Companions

Some games may feature relevant themes and at the same time have the creative bandwidth to allow developers to add pets or other creature companions. This opens up the freedom for the developers to introduce a wide variety of cosmetic variations to the pets and may even evolve into having sub-components to the pets which can be customized by the players.

Patterns, Stickers and Decals

These are often included within driving or similar games which center their customization around vehicles or equipment. The customization systems within these games allow for decorations such as stickers to be applied to the main body of the vehicle. Pre-defined locations are common, but many contemporary games allow the player to freely manipulate the size, shape and position of such objects.

Colors

Often, a game with a deep customization system will allow the player to apply color to certain items or areas of items. These could potentially be applied within or alongside patterns and decals.

Premium In-Game Stores

With the introduction of microtransactions that the player can make after their original purchase or download of a game, the game needs a designated area to arrange and promote content to sell to the player. In-game stores are put together in relatively similar fashions across different games. They must be easy and appealing to navigate, arranged to promote the best deals, and be kept updated with content that is interesting to players. It is inevitable that premium stores will expand as fresh content is added to the game, but clutter or too much choice can be detrimental to player spending. The following covers the different components and some of the best practices you can observe when managing premium content and store design.

Bundles

The use of bundles is a strong strategy for improving revenues, and bundling applies effectively to cosmetic vanity items that are part of many games. A bundle takes multiple items of content, packages them together into a single purchase and prices it at a percentage lower than the total value of all the items in the bundle.

The theory behind using bundles is that they allow players to see different value within the variety of content in the bundle, based on their personal preference. For example, for a first person shooter game, players will enjoy using different types of weapons within the game, which in themselves serve various strategic purposes, but certain players will have a preference for using certain weapons. Some players will choose submachine guns, while others will have a preference for using shotguns. A bundle with a submachine gun and a shotgun will appeal to both sets of players, with the players who prefer submachine guns seeing the main value of the bundle in the submachine gun and likewise players with a preference for shotguns perceiving the value in the shotgun. The bundling approach allows developers to ultimately sell more content to more players.

There are other related applications of bundles within monetization. Games which support high-end cosmetic items as part of their personalization strategy use bundles to sell collections of similarly themed content to players. For example, a game may include a bundle of items all themed after the dark web in their appearance. These items are only ever sold as part of the bundle and are created specifically for this purpose. These types of bundles can be used to package seasonal content, such as a Halloween bundle, or licensed cross-over content from other games or media.

A special case of bundle usage is the concept of the *starter pack* or *conversion bundle*. A starter pack would be a bundle promoted to players as an appealing way to spend within a game for the first time.

The usage varies depending on the design of the game. For a game with a purely personalization strategy, the starter bundle could involve a direct, real money purchase bundle, giving the player some cosmetic items and hard currency. The cosmetics would be visually premium, but not of the absolute highest quality. The hard currency would give the player the wherewithal to acquire more cosmetic content after this initial purchase. In turn, this coaxes the player into topping up this hard currency balance via further spending. Essentially, it helps to break the barrier to acquiring cosmetic content in general, encouraging repeat spending.

More complex and imaginative strategies can be employed with starter bundles. For example, they can be tied to seasons, and updated when the seasons advance, providing new content for players.

Discounts

Implementing a system for running discounts within in-game stores is imperative for when you are running live operations on any video game project, and this is even more important given the rise of games as a service. It is essential to build a generic system for controlling discounts from a game's backend systems, which can be applied to any item. Typically, the following settings will be required:

- The discount start time
- The discount end time
- The percentage reduction in price

When the discount is active, within the in-game store the normal price will appear scored out, with the discounted price next to it. There will typically be a widget showing the percentage reduction, along with a timer showing the time remaining before the discount expires.

The timing for activating discounts is about finding a "sweet spot" in terms of sales. If the discount is activated too soon after the content enters the game, players will latch on to this and simply wait for the discount, never buying items at their full price. Alternatively, if items are left in the store too long without being put on discount, money is left on the table as players will not spend as much as they would if the item had been discounted.

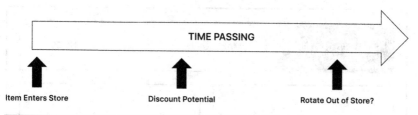

Figure 4.2   Diagram showing a loose plan for discount and item rotation over time.

After a game is live for a length of time and has included numerous updates, an in-game store cannot realistically support the inclusion of hundreds of items of content, and this can also become counterproductive to monetization. Therefore, there must be a strategy to remove items from the store. In general, after an amount of time has passed (one year is a sensible starting point), items can be tagged as having the potential to rotate out of the store. These items can go into a pool of old content and can be used for different purposes, such as being brought back into the store for special promotions (Figure 4.2).

Featured Pages and Promoting Content

An effective in-game store will include a variety of content, and there are many bespoke methods for arranging this effectively for players. It is important to place certain items within the eye line of the player and to take opportunities to highlight certain content. An effective approach for this is to utilize a featured page or similar within the design of the store.

The featured page will be a landing page for the store and gives developers the chance to place different promotions there. This can be used to display things such as new content or special licensed content. This area can also be used to highlight special weekly offers. If the game has larger expansion packs in the form of downloadable content (new story sections), then the featured page from the store can include adverts and links to this content (Figure 4.3).

Context–Sensitive Purchase Popups

The term "context sensitive purchase pop-ups" is my own invention. The concept can be seen within different games, but there is no convention for this design and no name associated with it. It is

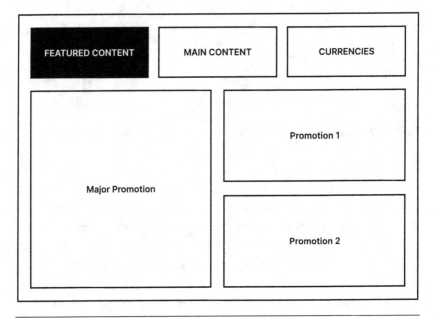

Figure 4.3   Basic mock-up of the UI design for an in-game store featured page.

nevertheless a powerful and aggressive monetization feature which can be used within an in-game premium store, to help provide the right offer at the right time for prospective buyers.

When the player visits the in-game store and attempts to click a Buy button on an item which is charged in hard currency, if the player does not have enough hard currency in their account, they will immediately see a popup, acting as an overlay on the current screen. This popup will show the player the smallest pack of hard currency that they can purchase in order to be able to buy the item they desire. The design will take into account the amount of hard currency the player has in their account, so the system will scan their account and offer the pack of hard currency that makes up the difference.

Pricing and Research

With the economy components defined as part of the game's design and lore, including the currencies, resources and goods, and the systems tying all these together, we must tackle the pricing of the content in relation to monetization.

As a rule of thumb, you will be looking to model the value of all the resources within the game to US dollars, even for the content that is not directly related to the monetization. Depending on the design of the game, you will always be linking this value to the time it takes players to progress through the game.

Here is where we must be mindful of the business models and the monetization strategies. For the performance and preference strategies, the pricing of content will be directly tied to the time that progress through the game takes. For soft currencies, you will be modeling the amounts of currency generated per unit time. It follows that the prices of monetized content in hard currency (which ties to real-world currency: US Dollars) can be balanced around the time that can be saved or the performance that can be gained from using the item once purchased.

For the personalization strategy, where the content is purely cosmetic, the value of the free/non-monetized content versus the monetized content is less connected. Therefore, to decide on the pricing of the premium monetized items, an effective place to start is to carry out a competitor analysis. This involves looking into other similar titles and delving into their pricing to gain insights into the standard pricing range for content across the industry.

To complement this, there are further strategies. Existing titles within franchises typically have a community, and new titles (hopefully) gain a community after launch. It can be worth leveraging this, by asking players and carrying out surveys on what are the most sought-after items. During the postlaunch period, it will be possible to analyze player spending data to gain knowledge of the most popular items and potentially adjust prices from there.

For the specifics of pricing in hard currency, it is common to use several different packs. We often refer to these packs as SKUs (Stock Keeping Units), since they are items that must be set up on the platform store's backend.

When defining the pricing of hard currency, it is initially pegged to US Dollars. Typically $1 would be equal to 100 hard currency as a base line, recognizable common practice. From here, the SKUs are defined with different pricing points. More hard currency costs more, but it is also demonstrably highly effective to give bonus currency for

Table 4.1   Pricing Table for Hard Currencies in USD, with the Percentage Extra Shown

PRICE (USD)	HARD CURRENCY AMOUNT	PERCENTAGE EXTRA
$4.99	500	0
$9.99	1200	20
$19.99	2500	25
$49.99	7000	40
$99.99	15,000	50

the higher tier price points. A typical example of a pricing table for hard currency would appear as follows, in Table 4.1. This uses five SKUs, although six is also common.

The table shows typical US Dollar prices and the amount of hard currency players get at each price, with $1 equal to 100 hard currency. Players are also gaining increasingly more generous bonus amounts, the more they spend.

Defining a minimum SKU price – in this case the $5 pack – requires careful consideration. This is largely dependent on the type of content that will be sold. Although there is no hard and fast rule, if the game typically involves cheaper purchases, such as upgrades within a free-to-play, performance strategy title, then it would be beneficial to have a lower cheapest purchase. It is also worth bearing in mind that if players tend to convert at the minimum price regardless, it can be beneficial to set it higher!

If the content in the game follows the personalization model which would probably center around selling higher priced cosmetic items, then it is important to include sensible price points which relate to this. It can pay off to be honest to players and certainly avoid forcing the player into buying more expensive hard currency packs in order to buy significantly cheaper cosmetics. To avoid this, you can, for example, charge 2500 hard currency for an expensive bundle, a straight up $20 purchase for the player in this instance. This is very transparent to players.

Analysis of the maximum potential spend possible within a game will be a consideration in defining the price points. This is known as the monetization cap and is an important part of the early design considerations when building an economy from the ground up.

Price Anchoring

You may be aware of the old adage from the world of advertising. "How do you sell a $2000 watch? Put it next to a $10,000 watch". This is the concept of price anchoring in a nutshell. The brain forms a cognitive bias whereby it takes the first piece of information and uses this to form relations and judgements for subsequent pieces of information. This can be used for pricing cosmetic items within a game, either with real money or with real money acquired hard currency. You can find ways to make certain items feel less expensive by placing them in the store alongside more expensive content. Anchoring also provides a way to set an initial high bar for pricing of content, for example for the most expensive legendary items, and all other content can derive lower prices from this point.

Decoy Effect and Compromise Effect

Related to the concept of price anchoring are two cognitive biases that are useful to consider: the decoy effect and the compromise effect. Both of these biases rely on a situation where an individual would typically be presented with the choice to purchase one of two alternatives, with the introduction of a third choice distorting the individual's perception of value of the original two, ultimately driving them toward the purchase of the seller's desired target item.

The Decoy Effect occurs when the seller presents the following to the buyer: a target product, a decoy product and a competitor product. This is best illustrated with an example. Suppose a drinks vendor is trying to sell orange juice. They offer the following products:

1. Small Orange Juice for $2.50
2. Medium Orange Juice for $6
3. Large Orange Juice for $7

The target product here is option 3, as it is only $1 more than the medium option 2, which acts as the decoy product, thus driving the buyer toward the better value of option 3. Option 1 serves as the competitor to the target product. Collectively, these three choices presented together make use of the decoy effect.

The compromise effect relates to the decoy effect, but differs in that the target is the middle option. Often this can be observed when selling different levels of services, such as subscriptions with a basic, standard and premium options presented to buyers, with more expensive options having more features. There is less appeal in buying the cheapest basic product with few features, and the premium option often seems unnecessary with too many features. Consequently, buyers are gently nudged into the standard option, the one that drives the most revenue.

Weber's Law

Weber's law is a principle which relates an individual's ability to perceive a change in a stimulus. Their ability to notice this change is related to the original size of the stimulus. This is best illustrated with the following scenario involving picking up objects of different weights.

If you were to pick up an object which weighs 2 kg, you would notice how heavy this feels. If you were then to add a small amount of weight to this object incrementally and continue to pick it up, there would be a point where you would eventually notice the difference in weight of the object.

If you were to then pick up an object which weighs 10 kg, you would notice that this, of course, feels heavier than the 2-kg object. If you were to, again incrementally, add small amounts of weight to it, it would require you to add more weight for you to eventually notice that the object has become heavier. In other words, for adding additional weight to two objects of different initial weight, the "just noticeable difference" (abbreviated to JND) is larger for the heavier weight than the lighter weight.

The JND is proportional to the original weight of the object. This is Weber's law, which is expressed as a formula:

$$\Delta I / I = k$$

where I is the size of the original stimulus, ΔI is the JND and k is the value which should remain constant. Therefore, with the weight example above:

Say that the 2-kg object requires an additional 0.2 kg added before a difference in weight is noticed.

$$0.2 / 2 = 0.1$$

We can work out that for the 10-kg weight, to attain the same value of $k = 0.1$, the JND must be 1 kg, as $1/10 = 0.1$

The example concerning weight is one among many, and Weber's law can be applied to numerous things in life, such as the senses. i.e. hearing, and various other things such as brightness, or how we perceive time passing.

Due to Weber's law, we perceive things in life logarithmically. In a generic sense, a small change to an initially small stimulus is felt much more strongly than a small change to a large initial stimulus. Therefore, for someone to feel a difference where a large stimulus is concerned, we would have to scale up the size of the change accordingly.

There are a large number of factors which play their part in affecting how we as humans notice stimuli, due to the complexity of the world around us and our sensory system, so Weber's law is only a guideline, but it has many applications across various industries. We should be able to see its relevance to game development and take it into account. In particular, relative to monetization within games, changes to pricing for content during the live operations of a game, and how players react to them, will certainly be affected by the kind of perception described by Weber's law. The developer must find a way to subtly increase prices, while seeking to minimize an adverse reaction from players.

References

Medium.com, Pricing Psychology: decoy and compromise effects, 2021. https://terrancereynolds.medium.com/pricing-psychology-decoy-and-compromise-effects-f78c9712f93f

Virtual Economies: Design and Analysis, Vili Lehdonvirta and Edward Castronova, 2014

5

Maintaining the Systems

Games as a Service

During the earlier days of the video games industry, before the internet was what it is today, video games were released on disc as products designed to give the complete intended experience to players. They were purchased, then consumed, after which players would move on and become engrossed in a new game. While this pattern of behavior still exists, a new type of long-term engagement has arisen, in conjunction with the expansion and efficiency of the internet: Games as a Service.

Games as a Service is a business model which involves a game that, after launch, is kept alive as a constantly evolving product with long-term development support from the studio. There are many games of different genres which are designed to be products with a "long tail" and are supported for many years post release. After the initial launch, the developer plans and schedules the release of updates to the base game, which will expand the content and potentially adapt the entire experience for players. This process goes under the heading of Live Operations and is a major part of game development.

For game economy designers in particular, working on a live game presents quite a different set of challenges compared to building a game economy from scratch during pre-production, through production, all the way to release. These processes bleed into each other and the work done during the period before launch must be carried out in a way that sets up the team to work efficiently on the product post launch. In general, we as designers work with the notion that we are constantly planning six months in advance, but in reality, we are planning for years in advance.

The term Games as a Service has a broad definition. Until this point within this book, the methods shared around economy and monetization design have been, by their very nature, part of the design for a game as a service project. Again, free-to-play titles are designed

DOI: 10.1201/9781003386865-6

around an intrinsic model of games as a service. This chapter will cover some of the approaches and tricks of the trade, for the work the economy designer must carry out after the project has launched.

Live Operations: Design Approaches and Considerations

The term live operations is, broadly speaking, the designation for all the work that is carried out on a project after launch. There are many parts to this, which concern all the different disciplines within game development. The technical team will be working on optimizations, improvements and bug fixes, which is a major, but entirely separate topic. The aspect of live operations with the most relevancy for the game economy designer relates to the new features to develop, and the ways in which we can manipulate the existing features to keep players playing, and spending money on the product for years to come. By the intrinsic nature of economy design work, the tasks you carry out long before launch bleed into live operations.

This section is very difficult to break down into specific rules. Not only do live operations differ heavily depending on the genre of game, but we also need to make peace with the fact that we are building a creative work. It is inherently unpredictable; players will engage with and react to a game's design in unexpected ways. Therefore, we must get the game into the hands of players, see how they react and then pivot or find a way to proceed with live design. We can absolutely have an idea of what we want to accomplish in the long term, but the key here is to remember there is no magic formula for the design and implementation of live game features.

This section covers some of the considerations with regard to the design that have specific relevance to the postlaunch phase of a game.

Cycling Content through the Economy

Digital goods which are distributed from within a game, such as cosmetic items and weapons, have a curious property, namely that they do not have the same natural obsolescence that real-world goods tend to have; they do not deteriorate in value over time from within the game. Nevertheless, entire games naturally do become obsolete as technology moves on.

From a theoretical standpoint, this lack of deterioration is something that does not facilitate building an effective and rewarding game economy. If a player has no reason to replace the content they own within the game as they play it, what motivation do they have to continue playing?

As a result of this, a certain type of obsolescence is often artificially built (or in a sense, forced), into the content. There are different ways in which games do this. For example, many games encompass a rarity system, the details of which are covered in Chapter 2, where the content is assigned to a category. Typical categories used are Common, Uncommon, Rare, Epic and Legendary. In the simplest sense, items of a lower rarity should be less powerful than items of higher rarity, although the specifics of how this is achieved must be tailored to the game in question.

As the player progresses through the game, completing missions, progressing the story, raising their level and increasing their skills, the economy will gradually distribute higher rarity content to the player to stay in synchronization with the challenges the game presents, which simultaneously renders the lower rarity content obsolete. This concept is something which can be generalized and used within the overall management of content and integration of monetization within games. Consider Figure 5.1.

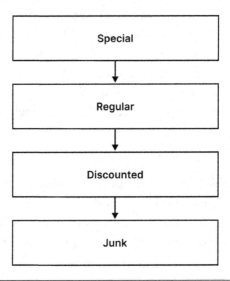

Figure 5.1   Diagram showing how content filters down through the economy in value.

This is a generalization, true, but it is a theory that we can loosely apply to whichever economy we are trying to build.

Content which is freshly added to the game is viewed as the most desirable and should be promoted as such. We want to draw the player's attention to this. This will eventually filter into the regular store, for example, as new special content is added to the game. When this content has been present for some time, we can boost its appeal with discounts, enticing players to make purchases. Finally, and although not applicable to every item, content may become "junk" and something which loses its appeal. However, the concept of junk in this context must not be taken at face value. Certain highly expensive items will never become worthless in the traditional sense, but there are many possibilities here. The items may be rotated out of circulation, or they may become replaced by others, for example, if items are shared across successive games within an ongoing franchise.

Purely cosmetic content with no gameplay impact is something which presents a different set of challenges. With regard to this, it is important that content is not all created equally. Even though there is the idea that cosmetic item purchases are associated with personal taste, it must be clear that some items are better than others in some way, as portrayed through the appearance of those items. For example, more expensive items can include special visual effects. As a game is supported long after launch, in an overall sense, the demand for better quality content increases, which relates to the idea of a content treadmill, covered in the next section.

Content Treadmills

Often, if you think of a popular title which has evolved and been maintained during the course of its postlaunch lifetime, the sheer volume of content that must be created requires vast amounts of money and development resources. There is always going to be a cost involved in keeping the live operations of a title going, but one eventuality for many games is that they become "content treadmills". Many development teams are not built to sustain games which become strong content treadmills, and they may not realize the work that will go into this.

The content treadmill is the idea that a development team must continually work to generate content to keep players engaged. During live operations and the lifetime of a game, the player's demand for new and interesting content keeps increasing, and the development team must work harder and harder, eventually struggling to meet player expectations, and in all probability running short on creative fuel. We can imagine a story-driven, episodic game as the epitome of the content treadmill. The main way to add value to the game is to add more content such as new story chapters. In this case, this is not necessarily a bad thing, but goes to illustrate the concept. However, for many other games, the content treadmill can be more insidious. This can become a factor for games which are sensitive to the idea of pay-to-win or pay-to-progress. Developers of these games, often reluctant to add mechanics or systems that have a functional impact on the gameplay, will attempt to monetize entirely through cosmetic content with the personalization strategy. This is a viable strategy, but tends to require expensive development resources to produce, and this only increases the more content that is required. The creative bandwidth related to whatever cosmetic content is viable can also become a factor. It is certainly possible to begin to introduce increasingly more outlandish cosmetics items into a game, the longer into post launch the title has been live. A game which starts off grounded in the everyday world can sometimes end up in a different universe after several years of development! However certain design and technical limitations can hinder purely cosmetic items.

Let's look at an example relating to the hypothetical Project X covered within this book. Considering this as a competitive multiplayer first-person shooter game, the team may decide to add emote animations which players can purchase via microtransactions. These emote animations cause the camera to switch to a third-person perspective, allowing the player to see their player character performing the animation. A side effect of this change of camera is that the field of view is now different, and players can use this to peek around corners in a way they normally would not be able to. These types of side effects are very regular occurrences during game development and form the normal problem-solving tasks of the game designer.

Considering the potential complications of going for a purely cosmetic monetization approach, what methods can the development team employ to move the project away from the content treadmill? It must be noted that there will always be some need to produce content. There is no magic solution, but the methods covered below can be considered.

Replayability of Existing Content There are many ways in which developers can inject replayability into their games. In fact, finding ways in which to give players a reason to replay a game, or parts of a game, is often a key goal and is credited as a positive attribute for any title.

One of the ways in which designers can achieve this is via the use of completion mechanics. These are typically systems which encourage players to go back and play a level, mission or certain sections of a game to attain some type of completion beyond the base requirements to pass that section. Some examples of this can be observed within action-adventure titles where optional items such as treasures are hidden within the game environment, but are likely to be missed on an initial playthrough. The player is therefore motivated to replay a section in order to collect all the treasures. Certain level-based puzzle games give players grades for completing levels, such as one to three stars. Highly efficient completion will give full three stars, which coaxes the player to replay a single level in order to fully master it.

Another way in which developers encourage replayability is to add elements of random variability to the game mechanics. For example, the enemy placement or even the structure of the environment can be procedurally generated, giving the player different experiences on each playthrough.

There are other creative ways in which old content can be given fresh appeal, for example, with a first-person shooter game where the weapons can be modified. New modifications can be added to older weapons, breathing new life into these weapons. While this still involves creating new content, it can give new ways for players to experiment and increase the gameplay value of weapons which they have already been using for longer periods of play.

Long-Term Upgrade Systems Depending on the overall design of the game, you can explore methods for stretching out the utility of the content by including systems whereby this content must be upgraded extensively as part of the gameplay. Many collectible card games or, in general, games which center around collecting hero characters or vehicles utilize these systems. The gameplay gives random resource drops used to upgrade whichever element the game is designed around, for example the hero characters which are collected. Progression through these upgrades to a final maximum upgrade level can be stretched out over long periods of time. First, the resources which are used to upgrade the items can have their distribution heavily controlled via the random drop chances. Building on this, multiple types of very rare resources can be used to control the upgrading further. *Marvel Contest of Champions* utilizes this system effectively, requiring the player to upgrade characters in distinct stages. Progressing past each stage requires the use of a special resource, in combination with the main upgrading resource.

Caution must be taken while building upgrade systems, as the system must fit with the type of game being created. I am continuously reminded of an example from my personal experience while considering this topic. I came into a project relatively late in the development process, when the core game loop had been implemented. Within this game, randomly dropped resources were used to upgrade weapons, boosting their statistics, such as damage, aim down sight speed and others. As a simple concept on paper, this objectively seemed to work well, but when put into practice within the project it did not provide a satisfying metagame experience. The problem lay in the fact that this type of upgrading system relies on the fact that the items which are being upgraded must be seen as distinct game mechanics in themselves. This works within games like *Clash Royale*, where each card being upgraded is a mechanic which has its own individual utility. In this case, the gradual upgrading of cards gives new ways for the player to play; they are building up their intertwined network of strategies and tactics by increasing the upgrade level of cards in a random fashion. However, within the context of a shooting game involving firearms as the object to be upgraded, these simply cannot be compared to cards with individual distinct properties. While the range of firearms included in different games certainly do favor different playstyles, they ultimately represent variations of similar styles of gameplay. As a result of this, there are natural limitations to the benefits that minor statistical upgrades give to these different weapons.

The ultimate result is that there is little benefit to stretching this upgrade process out over long periods of time, with end-game players not gaining sufficiently more meaningful upgrades in comparison to early game players.

In terms of the overall long-term user journey, there is a natural order in which players engage with the game, and therefore you can introduce specific later-game features to expand the player's utility with the game. Take a standard action-adventure title, such as the later entries in the *Uncharted* series, as a reference point. The game is mainly enjoyed as a single player, story-driven title, but includes a multiplayer mode. Although there is no restriction on players joining multiplayer whenever they like, they will spend only a finite amount of time on the single player story, and potentially hundreds of additional hours on the multiplayer mode, long after they are done with the story. In this sense, the player uses up the story content, and the multiplayer content can be seen as something which supports longer-term engagement. There are other methods in which games use specific end-game content, such as end-game raids within role-playing games, where experienced players are promoted to play together to defeat very powerful boss characters. These raids can often be repeated many times in the search for rare rewards.

One final point to note regarding content treadmills: there are two design approaches, covered in previous chapters, which can be used in the fight against the content treadmill. First, the use of a rarity system to artificially expand the content, closely integrated with the game's core design is a potential route. Within games which involve collection of loot as a central theme – for example, a looter shooter game – the same art assets can be re-used with the rarity system. These games can create (typically five) individual items out of a single art asset, with each item involving statistical changes and minor UI updates. These items can then be distributed in a controlled fashion, governed by the game's progression system, to create a long-lasting experience.

Second, the concept of an energy system is a way for designers to limit the content consumption of the players. While this can only be applied to the free-to-play business model and is potentially cumbersome, it can be a powerful way of putting full control in the hands of designers.

Soft Currency Inflation

You may be familiar with the colloquial term "a license to print money" which is often used to describe a very lucrative activity. Within video games, the main player activities which are repeated during every session, such as killing monsters or completing matches, are to all intents and purposes a license to print money. This tends to mean that if you introduce a liberally awarded soft currency designed to be used as a main base reward for everyday engagement, it will inevitably inflate. Even with careful planning, appropriate sinks and highly effective balancing, these currencies can be very hard to keep within reasonable amounts. There will be too much money chasing too few goods.

This raises the question of what the designer should do to tackle this problem.

First, it must be stated that you should approach this problem with the idea that it should be mitigated only. Searching for a perfect solution is not a viable aspect in metagame design, or in any aspect of game design. According to the general best design practice of making game economy systems at which you must be able to win or fail, the very fact that the soft currency can inflate is a sign that players can succeed at the game. There is also the fact that the development team has only limited resources and budget to produce content that the soft currency is used to purchase.

One method to combat this inflation is to look for ways in which you can introduce "infinite" sinks into the game. The infinite sink is one that can, in theory, be used an indefinite number of times without some type of hard limitation on its use. Selling cosmetic items which are owned permanently is a sink which cannot be re-used, but selling a consumable health replenishment item is a sink which could be used repeatedly for the player's lifetime with the game. If you can come up with extremely useful consumable items, then these will be something that players will spend their soft currency on and can become effective sinks. There are other costs which can be entered into a game's economy, such as taxes on buildings within the game (for a strategy game), or entry fees (charged for starting certain game modes) which are also worth considering, always respective of genre.

Other solutions to soft currency inflation are rooted in the idea that it is, as another best practice, far easier to use specific currencies for the different areas or modes of the game. For example, if there are

social features within the game such as player guilds, you can introduce a specific guild currency related to this and tie it to the gameplay
and content related to gameplay involving the guild. For mobile free-
to-play games, again respective of genre, it is far more acceptable to
use multiple currencies than with other titles, so this is something to
bear in mind. However, during live operations, as your main currency
inflates, you can allow this to happen and move the player to different
modes of the game and introduce new currencies to go with them.
Having multiple currencies and specific resources will make your life
easier when it comes to balancing.

While working on PAYDAY 3, the problem of rampant cash inflation was a significant issue which the team was tasked with addressing. The game is themed around heisting, so inherently the player
expects to be stealing large amounts of cash (soft currency). It would
not be a heisting game without this, and it feels good to end a heist
with large numbers summarizing your performance, appearing on the
payout screen. The problem arises with the fact that there is only a
finite amount of equipment, items and cosmetics that we could create to allow the player to spend this cash. There is also the fact that
there is a potential bandwidth limitation on how much to charge for
this content. We can only apply the logic of "It's a game!" to a certain
extent and charge vastly exaggerated amounts of soft currency. And
there still must be a discrepancy between very cheap cosmetics such
as colors and more expensive items such as new weapons. Ergo, some
content must have a relatively low price in relation to the amount of
cash the player is generating by playing. The game very naturally gives
rise to rampant soft currency inflation.

The feature the team implemented to try to combat this inflation
involved the use of a secondary currency, called C-Stacks within the
context of the game. The design of the C-Stacks is loosely inspired
by reserve currencies within real-world economies. The C-Stacks
are designed as a later game currency, distributed to the player in far
smaller amounts than cash. Through a special system within the in-
game store, the player converts their earned cash into C-Stacks, at a
rate which increases with each purchase, causing successive C-Stack
purchases to become very expensive, removing large amounts of cash
from the economy. The rate resets at the start of each week, so it is
entirely possible to wait and purchase at a cheap rate, but this rapidly

becomes very inefficient, and it is very easy to repeatedly buy C-Stacks at higher prices. Players must work hard to unlock content for purchase through the game's main progression systems, so once this content is unlocked and available for purchase, the C-Stack cost becomes something of an inconvenience, easily bypassed by spending a larger amount of cash. This is a far less daunting proposition than waiting for several days for an exchange rate to drop and nudges players into using this sink to remove cash from the game.

Fusion Systems The loose term "Fusion System" is typically used within game design circles to refer to a system whereby items are consumed to give some boost or benefit to another item. These systems are usually included in various guises within games which involve players collecting a large amount of different items, weapons or characters as a core part of their design. This can be typically prevalent in looter shooter games, certain role-playing games or gacha games. Within these titles, the player will end up with an inventory which is full of many weapons, potentially even many duplicates. In turn, these become redundant because they become greatly underpowered as the player progresses and finds new, more powerful items.

This situation gives the designers the opportunity to introduce a fusion system which serves the purpose of removing some of these items, while at the same time costing the player an amount of soft currency.

As a generic example, if a player has a surplus of weaker weapons, using the fusion system, they can merge an amount of these weak weapons with a more powerful weapon, which will boost the powerful weapon's stats. This process can be carried out with a soft currency charge, usually variable depending on the type of fusion occurring.

This system is powerful in that it is a sink for goods and a sink for soft currency simultaneously, and it also gives players a pleasing element of choice within their gameplay. Players may find a weapon, item or character that they particularly like, and thus the developer can use the fusion system to breathe new life into this content.

Planning Content

Content in the form of different items is a key aspect to many games. My main consideration in this section involves content planned out for games that contain a catalog of cosmetic items sold as part of the monetization design for a game. This includes cosmetic items created as part of a launch catalogue of items, but chiefly extends to items which are planned out as part of a live game. It is important to keep track of items which are in production and scheduled to be included within certain updates that occur at specified time intervals when a game is live. An important aspect to consider here is the fact that certain content must be patched into the game, while settings related to this content can be changed manually (or automatically) via backend servers, so the changes can appear instantly to the player.

To break this down a little more, if you need to add items to the game which must be stored locally on the player's device, then these will typically be added to the game with an update. This is something that you will have observed many thousands of times while playing a game: waiting for the latest version of the software to install. However, it also has an impact on the production process, as this kind of content must be scheduled to be included in the game in advance and must be appropriately planned.

On the other hand, certain aspects such as properties of the content, including the soft currency prices can be modified with the backend systems allowing you to change prices "on-the-fly". The changes will be made and then appear instantly in game when set to go live, without the client side update. There are different types of backend solutions for games, and there are third-party companies who work with game developers to provide their complete backend solutions.

Keeping track of a large amount of content will be part of the development process. This is a considerable task, which will typically be subdivided into smaller tasks. For example, a first-person shooter game will have an array of different weapons, but also possibly a catalogue of cosmetic items. These are two different sets of items which must be tracked and will be owned by different developers, potentially different departments, and will have a set of different stakeholders. However, all games require content so the following section will try to apply a general idea of how to manage this.

To plan out what items you are going to need for a game, let's take the example of cosmetic items which will be part of the monetization and mainly charged through an in-game hard currency (HC).

Using your preferred spreadsheet software, it will be helpful to create a document which resembles the following:

Table 5.1   Spreadsheet Mock-Up for Recording Cosmetic Content Planned for a Game

	A	B	C	D	E	F	G
			PLAYER FACING NAME		PRICE (USD)	PRICE (HC)	
1	INTERNAL NAME	TYPE	NAME	RARITY	(USD)	(HC)	SUGGESTION/DESCRIPTION
2	cosmetic_sticker1	Sticker	Comet	Epic	$0.99	100	Stylized comet with tail
3							
4							
5							
6							

For the cosmetic items within the game, you will need to keep track of these, and keeping a master-list of content in this fashion is one effective way. Please note that there is no fixed correct or incorrect way to record this information, and, as has become a recurring theme for much of this book, there will be different requirements depending on the project and the team working on said project. Table 5.1 shows an example snapshot of the fields needed, and there will almost certainly be more relevant pieces of information to track, though this kind of table will be a solid starting point.

The fields that you will need to keep track of will contain relevant information for all stakeholders, to be shared and maintained as content is created by the art and tech departments. New items will require an internal name to be used within the backend settings and/or within the development tools which the team uses. An important distinction must be made during the entire development process between internal names and player facing names. How this distinction is managed can cause confusion, and that confusion is often a point of learning for developers. Internal names are defined long before the final art assets are created, and it is a good practice to keep these internal names recognizable and relevant, but not necessarily connected to the actual appearance of the art asset. For example, for a cosmetic sticker item, you could go with the name "cosmetic_sticker1" or something along these lines. The reasons for this are that it will be far safer and cause less confusion in the long run, because the end result of content produced can be quite different to that which may have been proposed in the initial stages. Keeping development smooth with recognizable names which the game code uses will be make everyone's life far easier in the long run.

On the other hand, player facing names will be the responsibility of the narrative team (or similar related disciplines). These have different purposes both creatively and technically. Not only do players actually relate to them, but these names must be taken and localized into many languages. As a result, they have different technical needs and different stakeholders and will be documented by other departments, namely narrative. Either way, from the perspective of content planning, keeping a master-list record is vital. This means that the internal names and player facing names can be cross-referenced.

Recording the rarity (quality) of items is naturally something to include, and loosely tied to this will be the price. It is best practice to model the value of all resources in US Dollars, and the price in HC is linked to this. Including a brief description or suggestion for the item is valuable. While in charge of monetization and economy, you will be a stakeholder, but it must be stressed that the appearance of the content lies within the art domain. Nevertheless, having a description for quick reference is helpful and could even be replaced with a thumbnail image of the item after it has been created.

To expand on this master-list spreadsheet, when it comes to planning live content updates, you will need to include information regarding the timings for production: dates for planning and getting content into the game.

The following columns can be added to the spreadsheet:

Table 5.2 Spreadsheet Mock-Up Showing Planning Information for a Game's Content

	A		H	I	J	K
1	INTERNAL NAME		PLANNED	APPROVED	ART DELIVERED	IN GAME
2	cosmetic_sticker1	Other Item Information…	Yes	Yes	Yes	No
3						
4						
5						
6						

Within each of these columns, you can record the information pertaining to the production process, as shown in the example Table 5.2. This is where the work you undertake will be highly collaborative with the production department, and this will also be sensitive to change. You may record months or more specific dates within these columns, or potentially simply data such as "Yes", "No", "Unclear" or similar. This is dependent on the teams and their structure, and as ever, common sense plays a part here (Table 5.2).

An important practical point to note is that the work which developers undertake should be production driven, meaning that production is effectively the department that manages tasks for developers. This record of content is used between yourself, in charge of monetization, and the production team, who work with your plan to define development tasks.

As the person in charge of monetization (and in the broader sense of economy and game design), you are acting as a product owner, where you keep the end user needs as a priority, while linking this to development, in order to maximize the value to be delivered to the players. You are essentially representing the optimal end goal for the product, while bearing in mind the technical and financial limitations. To this end, you work with production who are more aligned with the practical realities of what can and cannot be delivered by the team.

Analytics

Before a game is launched to the world, there are several strategies for deciding on the values which control the distribution and consumption of currencies, resources and goods, the balancing values associated with the sinks and sources built into the economy. We can use spreadsheets and combine this with information gained from playtesting sessions. This can come from internal testers, but also from alpha and beta tests carried out with subsets of the final player base. Certain games also soft launch in several territories before their final worldwide launch. In any case, we often find that once a game launches globally, players behave in unexpected ways, and we must make adjustments to the balance of the game. This is the point where analytics comes into play. Designers will work with the analytics team to monitor player data and gain insights into how their designs are being engaged with by players. This means that they are then able to make informed adjustments.

To facilitate this during the development process, telemetry will be integrated into the game from a technical side. This will transmit data from the players who engage with the game to a database, which will then be turned into useful information for the development team.

Analytics is in itself a large topic, which goes far beyond the scope of this book, and is a separate career path for many, but since it is very useful for designer to have some knowledge of the basics, the following definitions and summaries will be helpful.

Metrics

Metrics in the context of video game analytics are numerical values used by analysts to evaluate the performance of a video game. There are many different metrics which developers can track, and these are used across all types of games and business models. Metrics are often specific to a particular project, part of the responsibility for which will fall onto the game design team. As detailed in Chapter 3 (Processes, Design Skills & Development Strategies), where the concept of analytics is integrated into a design from the ground up, the designer while specifying the feature they are working on, must identify aspects of this feature that can be tracked to give useful information about the feature's performance. This involves collaborating with the analytics department during the implementation phase.

For example, for a multiplayer first-person shooter game containing cosmetic real money purchases, the designer would be interested in tracking the number of sales of different cosmetic items, to aid future decisions on items that are selling well compared to those which are not. The art content team can then focus their efforts on creating vanity items which they know have greater appeal to the player base.

As a second example, consider a player-versus-player game with an account level which all players "level up" through as they put more hours into the game. The average account level a player reaches, relevant to the number of hours they have spent within the game, will be of interest to the economy designer, or indeed any designer working on the meta systems for this project. Having knowledge of this relationship between player level and time-in-game will help the designer to plan out the content and features which must become available to players to hold their interest.

Along with project specific metrics, there are other metrics commonly known to be applicable across every game, typically within the free-to-play mobile game development side of the games industry. These are known as Key Performance Indicators (KPIs).

Key Performance Indicators

Below are breakdowns of some of the key metrics of which game developers, especially game economy designers, should have a working understanding. A legitimate question which often arises is what would be good benchmarks (or average target numbers) for these metrics for a particular product. This is something that is very much dependent on the genre of game and the business model involved, and these benchmarks will certainly change as the games industry evolves. I feel therefore that it would be unproductive and unhelpful to try to include this type of specific information as part of this chapter. For an idea of these benchmarks, it is generally more prudent to use Google, check reports from analytics companies or possibly gain access to this information from a source within a development studio or publisher relevant to the project you are working on.

Daily Active Users (DAU)   The Daily Active Users is the number of unique users who start a session within an application, within a 24-hour hour period. The DAU is essentially a snapshot in time of the number of players playing the game on a given day. It is an important, staple metric for knowing simply how many players are playing a game and is used in conjunction with other metrics to gain further insights and calculate other important metrics. Monthly Active Users (MAU) is a related metric, which naturally functions in the same fashion, but considers a month-long period.

DAU/MAU (Stickiness)   The ratio of DAU to MAU takes the Daily Active Users and divides it by the Monthly Active Users. This metric, expressed as a percentage, is a good measurement of how well a game retains its users and is often referred to as "stickiness". We can illustrate this with a simple example. Say an app has 100,000 Monthly Active Users and 20,000 Daily Active Users. The DAU/MAU would therefore be 0.2 or 20%. Many companies would use the average DAU over a month, along with the MAU to get a feel for how many of the monthly active users are engaging with the app on a daily basis.

Sessions   A session would be defined as the user opening the application on their device. This does not need to be a unique user, but is simply any user. We can look at the number of sessions per DAU, which can give us an idea of how engaged the average user is with the application, and if they keep coming back to play again and again. In general, this metric is typically more associated with the mobile gaming space (though definitely not exclusively so), as mobile games are inherently designed around short sessions, and their design is built more around systems for coaxing users into repeated short sessions. By extension, some genres of mobile games will also lend themselves to a higher session count.

Retention   Retention is a very important key metric for free-to-play games, especially in the mobile space. There are several different types of retention which developers can track, though the most prominent which will be encountered are *Classic Retention* (sometimes called Day N Retention) and *Rolling Retention*.

For Classic Retention, we tend to look to Day 1, Day 7 and Day 30 as common benchmarks for applications. To explain these, consider the term Day 0 as referring to the day the user installs and launches the application. Therefore, if for example 100 users install and launch an application on day 0, and 40 users return to the application exactly seven days later, the Day 7 retention would be 40 out of 100 or 40%. The definitions for Day 1 and Day 30 follow from this. Classic Retention only considers users who return exactly on the Nth day specified after Day 0. Another type of retention measurement is Rolling Retention, which considers users who return to the application on Day N or later. The distinction between these two can seem subtle, but the impact on the retention data is significant. In fact, it is entirely possible to make poor decisions about a project by looking at Rolling Retention instead of Classic Retention. Rolling Retention will be naturally higher than Classic Retention, but the main drawback of Rolling Retention is that it can seem to change constantly. If a user returns to an application many months (e.g. over 100 days) later, all the previous Rolling Retention measurements will increase. For the vast majority of cases, Classic Retention is the metric which should be used, as it will give a more accurate, and unchanging percentage of users who returned to an application on a specific day, which when looking back on retention changes over time will allow developers to analyze their application's performance more effectively.

While D1, D7 and D30 are commonly used, there is evidence to suggest that longer-term retention is highly valuable, though analyzing retention for much longer periods after D30 presents problems. It is very hard to measure the impact of any changes you make if they only take effect many months after you implement them.

Churn Rate   The Churn Rate is the opposite of Retention. From the users who have installed an application, how many have now uninstalled it? This metric, like retention, also considers a time period. Considering the retention rate example above, if the day 7 retention is 40%, the equivalent churn rate would be 100% − 40% = 60%. Developers are interested in the reasons why users churn out of their applications. Early churn can be an indicator that the onboarding phases are potentially too complex and poorly designed. Churn which occurs after a week or more could be an indicator that there are issues with the deeper features of the application. For example, not enough new content is being unlocked to keep players interested. Churn can also be due to technical problems such as crashes and hangs.

Conversion Rate   The conversion rate is a monetization-related metric, applying chiefly to free-to-play games. During a specific time period, the conversion rate shows the percentage of unique users who make at least one in-app purchase, out of the total users for the same time period.

Despite the relevance to free-to-play, there are many games which include additional in-game or in-app purchases after the initial base game purchase (Referred to as the "Paymium" model). The conversion rate can be applied to these users as well, i.e. user who make further payments after an initial base game purchase.

Average Revenue Per Daily Active User (ARPDAU)   The ARPDAU is one of the most valuable KPIs of an application. This metric tells you the average amount money your game generates across each daily active user. ARPDAU can include revenue from individual sources such as in-app purchases or advertising or can be shown to include all revenue sources collectively. This in turn means that you can and should test and iterate on different monetization strategies. ARPDAU is an important metric to use to see the fluctuations in revenue which occur after updates and changes and is useful to monitor your project day to day. Drops or rises in ARPDAU will be easily apparent in the data in the short term. For a longer-term view of monetization, we can consider Lifetime Value (LTV).

Lifetime Value   The LTV metric has different methods of calculation and can be used across various industries. Some methods are more complex than others, but one relatively simple method, albeit one which is also considered to be only a rough estimate, is to multiply the ARPDAU by the User's Average Lifespan. In a formula this would be LTV = ARPDAU * Average User Lifespan. Calculating the Average User Lifespan can be established by using Retention data and by extension the Churn data. The LTV allows you to see how much money each user will generate for the game and will not only be helpful in testing content updates (as with ARPDAU) but will show a longer-term effect and can be a useful rough estimate of a game's profitability.

Average Revenue Per Paying User (ARPPU)   The ARPPU takes a sub-segment of the player base, those who have spent money within an application, and shows the analyst the average spend amount of those users. This metric considers the specific performance of the monetization strategy for a game, focusing only on the subset of users who are paying. As the vast majority of players within the free-to-play space will not pay, this metric becomes important as an indicator of how much engaged players are willing to pay and can give developers insights into the effectiveness of their pricing structure. It is also worth noting that this metric is largely genre dependent, and certain hardcore games will typically have higher ARPPU values.

Gaining Valuable Insights

The above KPIs are all valuable to know, and they can give us some insight into how well, or not a game is performing. We can gain high-level information, and as an economy designer, during the live operations of any application, you will find an important part of your daily work involves looking into this type of data. Theoretical knowledge is valuable, but for the purposes of forming a strategy to improve a product post launch, where there are a lot of unforeseen setbacks (and successes), as well as unpredictable player behavior, it is necessary to take a more pragmatic approach.

As game economy designers we must dig deeper and use these initial KPIs as a starting point, but then delve into specific metrics related to our game. This is the most effective way to obtain valuable insight into player behavior, which we can then use to modify and improve our project, and address potential problems.

When working on a game, it is important to gather worthwhile data on what content is being purchased by players and what is not. This will provide a foundation for deciding on the type and theme of content to add to the game to maximize monetization. Other useful data related to this will show how players behave within the in-game store if one exists. What are players clicking on first when they visit the store? And how does the placement of items within that store affect the purchases?

Analyzing the usage of certain content can provide insights into how players are behaving and potentially how this has a knock-on effect on the purchasing of premium content. It is essential, for example, to look into the usage data of weapons within a first-person shooter game. What weapons are players using the most? While certain weapons are naturally different from others in terms of their gameplay style, such as assault rifles and shotguns, other weapon types are more similar, such as assault rifles and submachine guns. Their distinction hinges on how they are balanced (considering rate of fire, damage, reload time, etc.). Therefore, if some weapons are not well balanced, they may become inferior and players will refrain from using them. Crucially, this type of information will reveal itself within the data from the player base. If, hypothetically, this game also includes premium versions of weapons, or simply skins for weapons which are paid for with real-world currency, the sales will be impacted if players are not willing to acquire and use the weapon in the first place. This is another example of the need for cross-collaboration of game economy design with other design disciplines.

It will also be imperative to study the player's use of currencies within the game. If a game includes a HC, which is mainly acquired through microtransactions, but also drops in small quantities via the gameplay, then as economy designer you will need to study the amounts players spend regularly. You will be able to get a sense of how much your premium content is worth to players based on how much progression-acquired HC the players spend on this content.

As you will be checking the main KPIs regularly to keep a finger on the pulse of how the game is performing, this will also give clues to potential problems within the game. For example, you may notice that the retention of a game shows a dip occurring at the seven-day mark. You then look into the experience levels that players on average attain after seven days of play. You notice that they are failing a particular mission at this experience level and are not getting a consistent cadence of rewards. This therefore constitutes strong evidence tying the lack of progression to the retention drop, and from here you can address this issue.

What Features to Implement?

We now have a basis for the strategy of live design covering the planning, the content and the pitfalls to avoid, while also considering the important topic of analytics and how the designer uses these. But to round off this chapter, let us look at a larger question related to the top-level game direction. Once a game is live, what features should be implemented to maintain player interest and strong monetization? This is yet another open-ended design question. There is not one size fits all but there are certain observations that can make things easier for the designer.

Certain development work will be assigned to the production of new content and expansions to existing features. For example, if the game contains a Battle Pass, new content must be produced to reflect that. Similarly, new content must be produced for an in-game store and other areas of the game. For a story-driven game, extensions to the main game story can be produced via DLC content.

New game modes and social features also form a major component of the work that will be carried out post launch. In terms of coming up with a strategy for how to approach these features, one useful method could be to consider the Bartle Taxonomy to try to understand what types of players the game caters to and how our knowledge of these types can be harnessed.

Every gamer is different in their habits and in the ways in which they enjoy video games. The Bartle Taxonomy is a classification of player types, which is based on a paper called "Hearts, clubs, diamonds, spades: Players who suit MUDs", written by Richard Bartle in 1996. This paper delves into the different aspects that players enjoy within Multi-User Dungeon games and abstracts this out to consider four player types: Achievers, Explorers, Socializers and Killers.

Achievers are players whose main aim is to attain a title's in-game goals; that is, to gain points, levels, treasures and similar objects. They are described as the "completionist" type of player who must do everything that a game offers and by doing this consider themselves to be succeeding at the game.

Explorers are players who are interested in discovering what the game has to offer, centering around finding new things within the game. This can range from digging deep into the systems to find out exactly how they work and even innovate within them, to exploring parts of the game's environment which few people will ever come across.

Socializers are players who play the game for its community and the accompanying interpersonal aspects of the game. They find their main enjoyment in meeting other players. These players are primarily those who will get the most out of the game's social features, such as the guild or clan systems within the many different multiplayer games on the market.

Killers are players who play the game mainly to dominate, competitively defeating other players. Typically, they find their enjoyment in the idea that they are causing some degree of grief to other players, derived (in most cases at least) from a friendly competitive spirit. These players naturally thrive in the player-versus-player games or modes, where they can assert this dominance over others. There are other ways in which killers come to the surface, such as through the drive to beat another player's record.

Achievers and explorers typically have a preference for interacting with the game world, while killers and socializers have a preference for interacting with other players. Secondly, killers and achievers tend to have a preference for one-sided action, compared to socializers and explorers who have a preference for interaction.

With these player types in mind, we can decide on different features which would be most effective in improving the game's experience for our players. If we find that we want to emphasize the social aspects of a game, and if this is not something that has come to the forefront from the initial launch, we might consider developing a player guild. Another eventuality is that we may discover that players feel the need for shorter sessions and want to gain quicker rewards. In this case, adding an Arcade Mode with quick-fire rounds of gameplay could benefit the overall experience. In this sense, it would probably please the "killers" as identified by the Bartle Taxonomy. Achievers, on the other hand, will probably find the most effective ways through to the end-game stages of the game economy, and at this point, adding features which give these players new utility can be highly effective in retaining their interest. These could be features such as end-game boss dungeons which must be grinded for rare treasures.

The main conclusion to draw from this is – of course – that not all gamers are the same. Not all gamers appreciate the same features of play for the same reasons. The more we, as economy designers, can learn about the nature of the relationship between the player and the game, the more effectively we can design a game economy to suit a maximum number of gamers and the more effective we can become in responding to the needs of our target audience.

References

Braze, "The Top 3 Ways to Calculate User Retention Rate with Formulas", 2016. https://www.braze.com/

Deconstructor of Fun, "Managing and Avoiding Content Treadmills", 2016. https://www.deconstructoroffun.com/blog//2016/09/managing-and-avoiding-content-treadmills.html

GameAnalytics, "15 Metrics All Game Developers Should Know by Heart", 2015 https://gameanalytics.com/blog/metrics-all-game-developers-should-know/

"Hearts, clubs, diamonds, spades: Players who suit MUDs", Richard Bartle, 1996.

What Games Are, "The Free-to-Play Triangle [Game Economics]", 2012. https://www.whatgamesare.com/2012/10/the-free-to-play-triangle-game-economics.html

6

GETTING INTO THE BUSINESS, WORK AND SKILLS

A quick Google search will turn up a great many articles giving advice about entering the video games industry. You will undoubtedly see patterns in the recommended steps you can take, and many of these articles contain solid guidance which, if followed, will move you in the right direction. Certainly, entering the games industry as a programmer or artist can be much more straightforward in terms of useful career advice and defining realistic workable steps to follow. Advice for entering the industry as a game designer will be inherently more vague. In reality, there is a less formal path for the aspiring designer, and much of the advice is actually realistic in the sense that it amounts to a checklist of things that you should do to swing the odds in your favor. Naturally this applies to game economy design as well, but there are certainly educational paths which lend themselves more effectively to the role, and these are the paths which I will cover in this chapter.

The first major caveat regarding advice on entering the games industry is that the field is constantly evolving (much like the games industry as a whole), and with ever improving vocational educational programs, I am confident that the routes into design will become more formalized in the future, which is a positive development.

The second major caveat is that following advice within this chapter, or from any source, is in no way a guarantee of finding work. You absolutely must put in the hours of groundwork and be willing to constantly learn new things. There is no magic wand to wave to get you into the industry.

This chapter will discuss the finer details involved in entering the games business and the steps involved in building a lifelong career in this fascinating industry.

DOI: 10.1201/9781003386865-7

Disciplines within the Games Industry

The numbers of game development teams working to create new and innovative experiences for players are vast. There are teams of varying shapes and sizes, from the lone developer, to studios consisting of hundreds if not thousands of people, covering many disciplines and subsets within these disciplines. Despite this variety, and the ways in which the games industry has evolved over the years, there are four core disciplines involved in game development which have remained largely consistent throughout the industry: Game Design, Programming, Art and Production.

Game Design

Game design, and its subspecialty of game economy design, is naturally the main focus of this book, and as a member of the design team, during any project you will collaborate regularly with members of the programming, art and production departments. There are other subspecialties of game design, and the role itself adapts depending on the size of team and project.

For small projects, there will be a lone game designer who will cover every aspect of game design. This is feasible with projects that are sufficiently small in scope. From my own background building up a micro studio, working as the sole designer was an interesting experience, and one in which the learning curve was steep, with a requirement to "wear many hats". In particular, being part of a work-for-hire studio, I was involved in the entire process of a project from the very start all the way to postlaunch support. This included collaboration with business development, meeting clients and analyzing project briefs from a game design perspective, and creating pitch documents.

With titles increasing in size and scope, teams expand, and design will separate itself into more specialized roles covered by different individuals. One such role is that of level design. These are the designers who physically lay out the terrain which players move through and explore when playing. It is worth noting here that level design has been recognized as a separate entity to game design for many years, and although there is some overlap, the level design team will often be separated out from the design team in practical terms during a project. There is a lot of sense to this separation, as fundamentally, a level designer is there to create interesting physical spaces to explore, but a game designer is more interested in the rules and loops of play which drive player engagement.

The larger the project, the more subdivisions of game design find their way into development studios and it's worth exploring and defining some of these subdivisions here.

Systems designers will cover different features within a game, for example gun play in a first-person shooter game. System designer is a fairly broad term in itself, and designers with this role will deal with many aspects of the game, including artificial intelligence and combat. In a sense, all game design can be thought of as a type of system design, but the name "system designer" is used when there are complex, relatively discrete features which need to be created for a larger project. At times, this job will be advertised with the specific area the designer is intended to cover within the job title. You may, for example, see adverts for combat designer appearing on company websites.

Narrative designers act as a central point for everything that is narrative related within the game. The job involves aspects of game writing such as creating storylines and writing dialogue for a game, although normally there is a distinction between these two roles. Narrative designers are responsible for working on the narrative aspects that arise from the systems that the system designers work to create. They will write and edit copy for characters, items and backstory, and work cross-department, for example with the art and sound departments, to help convey the story aspects of the project.

The term content designer may also be used. Considering the extremely subjective, project-dependent nature of game development, I have found that, in practice, many of these roles cover much the same development tasks. Certain genres lend themselves to creative content more than others. Role-playing games typically require a huge amount of content related to quests, non-player character dialogue and equipment. This is where the content and narrative designer comes to the fore.

Technical designers are part programmer, part designer. The technical designer works with the pipeline of the project, acting as an interface between the design and programming teams, to assist in turning the system designer's work into a tangible, working artifact within the game. The technical designer assists the game design by solving problems related to workflow, software and tools.

User interface designers tend to blend game design with aspects of art. In essence, they may not be fully fledged artists, but will often need to use special software to prototype the game's menu screens and specifically the user's journey through these screens. UI designers cover UI elements that, for example, appear in the heads-up display for the in-game screens, along with the multitude of front-end menu screens.

As we have seen in the preceding chapters, the way in which game economy and monetization designers fit into the industry as a whole will vary, depending on the size of the studio and the nature of the game in development. Game economy design is a subspecialty of design overall, but you will need to be aware of the various other design roles in order to fulfill your function as economy designer both efficiently and creatively.

We now move onto the other three core disciplines.

Programming

Programmers write the lines of code that make the game work. Programmers are sometimes referred to as "engineers" within the games industry. The programmer's job is to *make things work at a technical level*. Programming has many subspecializations including gameplay programming and network programming to name but a few. Programmers will build the systems that you, as the designer, have specified. This cross-collaboration with the engineer providing a technical solution to a design problem is a major aspect of working as a game designer. Some programming specialties have more of an impact on the player's experience than others. Naturally a gameplay programmer will be working on the aspects of a game with which players directly interact. While it can be beneficial for the game designer who works with a gameplay programmer to have program-ming knowledge, it is conversely essential for this type of programmer to have an interest in the design of the game. Through experience,

I have known some programmers to have a knack for implementing systems which are fun for players and reflect the design but also have some extra creative flavor and thus have a positive impact on the player's experience.

Art

Artists use software such as *Maya* or *3ds Max* to make the art objects that players see in the game. There are again many subspecialties within art, such as environment art, concept art, visual effects art and more. As game economy designers manage the in-game goods and content, there will again be some cross collaboration. In particular, in a game where the long-term goal involves collecting and upgrading various weapons or equipment, or a game with an array of cosmetic content designed to allow players to show off their unique style, you will find yourself providing a degree of direction for the creation of this content. This may involve conveying the needs of the game to senior staff within the art department, and providing feedback and working with artists to organize and get this content into the game during the development process. However, in reality, you will work more closely with programmers than with artists during your day-to-day work as a designer.

Production

The production department within a game development studio looks toward the big picture of a project. Producers oversee the development of a game from concept to release. They manage the teams, and the project timeline, to keep it on schedule, thus ensuring that the product is delivered within the allocated budget and to the required level of quality. Members of the production team covering different areas will coordinate with the main development disciplines: game design, programming and art, while also having a working relationship with many other areas of the company, including quality assurance (QA), marketing and business development. The relationship between design and production is a complex one, and members of the production team will spend a lot of time and energy working together.

Within the design and production relationship, designers will be in charge of the creative needs and finer details of features, with the work itself being driven by production. Once again, we can see that the games industry is highly collaborative, a quality which it shares with many other creative industries.

Education

This section is primarily aimed at those who are still in high school, with a passion for video games, and who are considering a career in the games industry.

When I was at the very start of my working life, around the year 2008, the routes into game design were much less well defined than they are today. This is not to say that education programs specifically tailored to design did not exist, but I cannot deny that beginning in the industry with the aim of becoming a designer required its fair share of luck as well as persistence. Vocational university courses have grown and expanded over the years, and now there are many more formalized courses for game design worldwide.

I still remember the single best piece of advice I was given, just before I began my degree, which was, at this stage of life, to keep my options open. It still seems like good advice, given that most of us leave school without being fully aware of the many options open to us. If you have a passion for games, and even if you think you know where you will best fit into the industry, I believe you should still not specialize too early.

The first thing you should be aiming to do is to get a degree level education. From my own experience, studying Mathematics has been invaluable for a career in game economy design. In general, I would recommend studying a relevant science degree, in particular Mathematics and/or Computer Science. The skills, knowledge and ultimately the thought processes developed through studying such subjects will form the basis of the work you will do when crafting game economies. As designers we are always thinking of systems, and how these systems interact with each other, with the effects of change in one system affecting another. Studying mathematics will undoubtedly help in how you visualize and process this key aspect of your work. Game economy design involves a lot of deep and complex problem solving, and the "mental state" you attain from spending your student years solving complex problems will stand you in good stead for the rest of your working life.

Even if you are not interested in a formal mathematics education, it is of course still possible to work as a game economy designer. However, I would like to dispel the enduring myth that certain people simply cannot learn mathematics. There is some truth in a natural aptitude for almost any skill, and of course a percentage of individuals will become more proficient than others with the same amount of training. However, mathematics can be learned. It requires a good teacher and regular practice to overcome the early frustration phase which deters many.

The other skill which is essential, and which is sometimes neglected, is a solid grounding in written communication. Designing games involves the creation of detailed documentation. With multiple teams covering different areas of game development, the need for written direction is inevitable, so learning to write well and clearly is the key to success. You will find that writing as a skill for game designers is widely accepted, whereas mathematics may be seen as a more specific skill for game economy design. As a side note, creative writing and scriptwriting are separate specialized writing skills which are not directly relevant to game economy design.

Entry-Level Roles

The games industry (along with many other industries) suffers from the well-recognized Catch-22 that an individual requires experience in order to get a job, but needs this job in order to get the required experience to begin with. This is a problem which is gradually being alleviated by the improving standard of vocational education in video game development. Education programs are often connected closely to the games industry, and as a result, internships and opportunities are instituted and actively designed for those with no professional experience, thus helping them to get their foot in the door. Even so, persistence and perseverance in the face of occasional disappointment or rejection can make all the difference between success and failure.

Internships and Junior Designer Roles

Internships are an excellent way to begin a career in the games industry. Though not every company provides internships, there are hubs of game development studios in different areas of the world, and educational institutes within these hubs. As game development courses tend to be – and will become even more – closely linked to development studios, these companies collaborate with universities and give placements to students, with the aim of offering eventual employment opportunities.

Employment following an internship would typically take the form of a junior design role. It is, of course, possible to enter the industry directly as a junior designer, This, however, is by no means a typical approach, mainly due to the aforementioned Catch-22. Without the benefit of an internship, finding a way into the design team via QA (see below) is typically a more realistic route. It is worth bearing in mind, even with an appropriate education, whether in a traditional academic subject or a tailored game-specific degree, that there is no fixed route into game design. A junior design job is generally considered a starting point, although depending on your background and the company's size and structure, there may be no strict hierarchy and the starting point would simply be as "game designer" on a small team or as the lone designer within a small company.

Game Testing

A common first rung on the ladder in the games industry is through the QA department within a game development studio. The main reason for this is that finding work in QA does not, typically, require previous experience in the games industry. It can even be possible to gain some QA work before graduating or as a possible summer job.

I believe that gaining some experience in the QA department is extremely important for aspiring game designers, regardless of which area of game design you are interested in. Game testers learn a great deal about the processes involved in game development, and the job itself leads into design arguably more so than into other disciplines. In many ways, a large part of game design involves testing and iterating on game systems as they are built, ergo some initial experience in testing games forms an ideal foundation for a future design career.

It is interesting to note that game economy design tends to lend itself to learning on the job, and when working in QA, you are able to interact with a professional game design team on a daily basis, so opportunities can be engineered. A student project, while extremely useful, tends to focus on a game's core mechanic in the form of a vertical slice, designed to be submitted alongside a resume as part of a job application. As the game economy designer is more concerned with the long-term engagement of a player, and adjustments based on player data, it essentially requires a fully built, professional project in order to demonstrate the designer's skills. QA will give you at least some of that required experience.

It is worth pointing out here that larger game development studios include testing departments, but there are also external testing companies, to which developers and publishers outsource work. For those who are looking for their break into the design team, working directly within a development studio will certainly provide more opportunities to interact with game designers and ultimately more realistic opportunities to join the design team. Nevertheless, some experience with an external testing company should not be rejected as a way into the industry, since the experience gained may make it easier to move into a larger game development studio.

Tips on Breaking into the Games Industry

Getting a solid education and exploring entry-level roles is a natural way for getting started, but the routes can be circuitous and difficult, and luck certainly plays a significant role in those early career stages. There is a lot to be said for being in the right place at the right time and for the stars to align! You could argue that luck plays a role in many aspects of working life across many careers, but it is also the case that luck can be engineered or at least fostered, and there are things that you can do to swing the odds of success in your favor. The following tips will not be accessible to everyone and may seem obvious to others, but there are certainly things that you can take into account and work with to suit your own needs and aspirations.

Read Books and Articles about the Games Industry

As you are reading this book, you are already on the right path in this respect. I recommend reading as much as you can about game design and the games industry as a whole. Of course it goes without saying that you will be playing games – but you should be reading about them too. The games industry is rapidly evolving and seems to be in an everlasting state of flux, and it is important to stay up to date with the constant evolution that is happening. Keeping up with new developments is vital. There are many sites covering the business and development side of the industry, and many people, journalists and academics alike, analyzing developments. I would suggest that you build up a habit of reading about the industry and staying as current as you can. The industry itself is so collaborative and so interlinked that whatever your future aspirations, being aware of and reading books and articles on game design and other disciplines will stand you in good stead for entering and progressing your career.

Network, Network, Network

It is true to say that attending conferences can involve spending an amount of money which, especially for a student or early career designer, can prove problematic. All the same, nine times out of ten I have found it to be money well spent. The main reason for this is the opportunity to network, forge industry connections and ultimately get to know developers who are hiring or may be doing so at some point in the future. The phrase "it's not what you know, it's who you know" is often true, even if many of us would rather not believe it. "Where there's a will, there's a way" can also be true. Some conferences have special rates or bursaries and inexpensive accommodation for students. Other funding may be available if you seek it out. Many conferences have networking and social events in the evenings, and these, or even low-key gatherings such as coffee breaks, can present prime opportunities to meet key individuals from the games industry face-to-face. Attending such a conference can be an invaluable experience, and showing your enthusiasm and abilities to the right person could be just the break that you require.

Put Yourself at the Heart of the Action

You may have heard the stories of a hypothetical aspiring actor who moves to Hollywood to pursue their dream. While it may be unrealistic for the vast majority of people, moving to this key part of the world may well be a very viable strategy for someone who wants to work in film. You need to put yourself in the epicenter of the action, the place where the industry thrives. Then, with the aforementioned luck and networking, opportunities may present themselves. This does not just apply to those entering the games industry for the first time, but for general career building over the long term. While remote working has grown and become far more commonplace, there will always be benefits to placing yourself geographically within the city or area where games companies are located. There are certain hubs around the world: San Francisco, Seattle, Stockholm and London to name only a few, but there are many others depending on your location. Personal circumstances and bureaucratic complications may make relocating to another country challenging, but the possibilities are there, and the games industry provides opportunities for this.

Promote Yourself

Once you have made your resume as good as it possibly can be, creating a presence online and within game development communities can be a useful and inexpensive activity. You can use all forms of social media, join communities, set up a website or blog, and starting writing about games and game design, focusing on whatever aspects most interest you, in an informative way. Don't be deterred by the sheer volume of material out there. Instead, try to find your own niche, be professional and keep your aims and aspirations in mind.

Solo or independent game development is not the subject of this book, but if you are someone who has programming and art ability and are interested in putting together small games, or if you are working with a group of friends to make games, this is also something which can readily help you to land a first job in the games industry at a larger studio.

Working as a Game Economy Designer

Congratulations! You've succeeded in obtaining a game economy design position. What next?

While undertaking a formal education within science subjects where problem solving forms the majority of the student's learning, certain aspects that the lecturers and tutors try to reinforce are the general best practices for solving a problem.

From my own days as a mathematics student at Glasgow University, I recall the lecturers giving clear instructions to us to make conscious attempts at the various weekly exercises, stating that you should be "banging your head against the wall" for at least 30 minutes, before considering asking someone for help. Similarly, I remember being warned against looking at solutions to problems before truly attempting them. After all, understanding someone else's solution to a problem is quite different from coming up with a solution of your own, although this understanding of a solution is useful in different circumstances, and part of the overall goal of improving problem-solving skills. This type of guidance from lecturers may seem counterintuitive and is certainly not to be taken to extremes. We are often told, sensibly, that we should never be afraid to ask for help. The trick, therefore, is in not asking for help too soon, but in trying to solve the problem by yourself first. Science subjects require consistent practice and training, and we tend to learn more by worrying away at a problem, rather than expecting somebody else to solve it for us. Game design is no different.

Another high-level technique for problem solving, which initially may seem contradictory to the notion of attempting something yourself, is the ability to recognize a problem that has previously been solved and re-apply the method used, even loosely, to another situation. This is a perfectly valid method of problem solving, and one which many of the examples contained within this book utilize to provide a foundation for designing many types of games. Re-using previously applied methods means that one should never seek to "re-invent the wheel", which can so easily become an exercise in wasting time and resources; the last thing a commercial game development project requires.

Bringing these notions of problem-solving techniques and best practices together, I believe the following general approach for a game economy designer should be as follows:

Begin by taking some time to think about a problem in a quiet corner. Although we all work differently, it can be beneficial to write things down by hand before going near a computer screen. From studying computer science for several years along with mathematics, I also remember being taught not to rush into coding, but to take the time to think through a problem by writing pseudo-code. This is a practice which you can take forward even for game economy design problems.

Following this, Google becomes the next port of call and is something you should also be considering in its own right as part of the overall research that you will inevitably do when faced with any task. It's now very unlikely within many professional fields that you are facing a problem that someone else hasn't also already faced, albeit in a potentially different guise. The solution to your problem may already be available.

Finally, if a problem is really presenting a significant blocker, you can consult with other members of the team or a lead. They may give insight or some way of circumventing the issue.

This strategy is only a general guide, but the key takeaways are not to instantly ask a colleague for help without first taking time to think for yourself, but never fear asking for help in the long run. Always remember that you can research and reapply proven methods. There is a fine balance to be achieved here and experience will help you to succeed.

If the working relationship between designers and programmers is something of an art form, then the working relationship between production (and/or project managers) and designers is even more crucial. On paper the disciplines are separate, but once a game development project is underway, the nature of both jobs will cause overlap in different ways. A game may be creative, but it must be completed within a time frame and budget, and the people working on the technology and art will affect the end-product massively. Therefore, the designer must be able to work with those who are managing this side of things. Likewise, for a producer to be able to do their job and drive forward the development efforts, they must have some understanding of what is involved with those efforts.

There will inevitably be a back-and-forth series of interactions between the designer and producer, along with members of the technical and art teams to create manageable tasks, recorded in project management software.

While game economy designers are interested in creating interesting gameplay loops, the user interface designers are interested in creating an attractive series of systems by which players interact with the product. In practice, this means taking a design and planning out the details of how the artistic user interface elements appear and how the menus and various other components function. The UI design discipline is linked to art, more so than other design subdivisions, due to ways in which games are made with art being somewhat of a "shell" on top of the game systems. This means that the UI components which are part of economy-related features are best left to the UI team to tackle without much interference.

References

Game Balance, Brenda Romero and Ian Schreiber, 2019
Gameplay and Design, Kevin Oxland, 2004

7

CASE STUDIES

I feel I need to qualify this chapter. Fully deconstructing an existing design is, in reality, quite different from building a system yourself as a practicing professional designer. During the development of a game project, there are many aspects which are conceived, designed, re-designed and cut as the project comes together. Also, there is a "human factor" during development; everyone who works on the project affects the outcome, and these people have their individual skills, mindsets and lives in general. When trying to critically evaluate a game, one that you have not worked on yourself, you can never hope to have access to all the development information under the hood of a project. This is not to say that taking time to deconstruct existing games is a waste of time. Playing and taking inspiration from many different games to learn and grow as a designer is very much a key part of building a long-term, successful career.

However, it's important to bear in mind that analyzing a game involves making deductions based on a final, public facing product. Considering there are many nuances and subtle minutiae involved in the process, you can only truly understand the behavior of a project's systems if you have navigated the development minefield of that project yourself.

I have chosen two games to look at: the mobile game, *Marvel Snap*, and the PC and Console game, *The Finals*. Both of these games are examined for different analytical purposes. First, *Marvel Snap* is a great example of an elegantly designed metagame and progression system. *The Finals* shows highly skilled product ownership over the monetization and in-game store.

Marvel Snap

I consider *Marvel Snap* to be a strong example of a free-to-play design with systems for long-term engagement which I deem very

DOI: 10.1201/9781003386865-8

clean and concise. There is a single core game experience that players take part in, and the meta systems of progression, resource acquisition and spending and ultimately monetization are built around this. There is also an interesting innovation whereby rarity upgrades have purely cosmetic effects, but in turn, feed into the overall progression.

Introduction

Marvel Snap is a free-to-play, mobile collectible card game. The game is player-versus-player, with players competing in battles against each other.

The matches are quick and conceptually straightforward to understand. Each player has a deck of 12 cards, with each card depicting a Marvel character with a power value, energy value and a special ability (if any). The play area is composed of three locations, each having different properties affecting the gameplay. Players take turns dropping cards onto the locations, with the power value on the card dropped increasing the power shown on the location. For every round there is a total energy value (increasing with each round) which limits which cards the player can use from their deck.

A match lasts six rounds, and the player with the highest power at a location after six rounds wins that location. To win a match, a player must win two out of the three locations.

Most of the cards in the game have a special ability, of which there are a multitude. An example of a special ability could be adding +2 power to all adjacent locations.

From this simple concept, the core gameplay derives its strategic depth through the synergy between the various special abilities associated with different cards and their energy value, with players building their decks around the different properties of the cards, essentially mixing and matching the special abilities of cards. It is important to be able to have strategic options early in a match where the amount of energy available to use is less, while saving more energy-consuming, but powerful cards for the final few rounds.

The long-term engagement is centered around collecting and upgrading cards, which will be covered in the following sections and is the central focus of this case study.

Core Loop

The core loop of gameplay within *Marvel Snap* is summarized by Figure 7.1, which comprises two main aspects, Battle and Upgrade. The player competes in battles with other players, which feeds into the metagame goal of collecting more cards, allowing for more strategic deck building.

Battle   The player takes part in battles against other players, using their own pre-selected deck of cards. At the end of each battle, the player gains an amount of Boosters for a randomly chosen card in their deck. Boosters are resources which are card specific and used to upgrade cards.

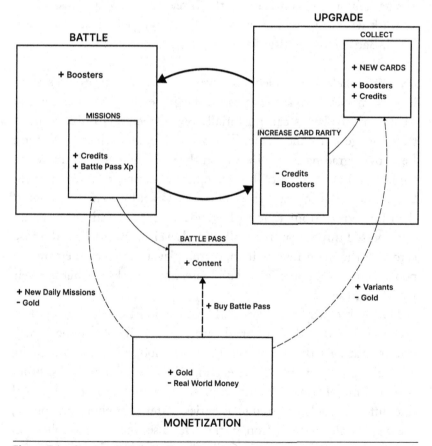

Figure 7.1   Core loop diagram for *Marvel Snap*.

Players will complete daily missions and Battle Pass specific missions also by engaging in battles, gaining experience points for the Battle Pass and amounts of the game's main soft currency, called Credits, which is used in tandem with Boosters to upgrade cards.

Upgrade   Players spend both Boosters and Credits to upgrade cards. Upgrading a card increases the card's rarity, which is represented by a more prominent cosmetic effect/appearance associated with the card. In turn, upgrading a card increases the player's *Collection Level*, which is the main progression track used to unlock new cards, amounts of Credits and boosters for randomly selected cards the player owns.

Progression Systems

The game's progression features the three following systems, which all work with a synergy to push the player's engagement: Collection Level, Battle Pass and Ranks.

Collection Level   The Collection Level is the main progression system which controls the player's access to the game's content, determining what content players can potentially own depending on how much they engage with the game. The player increases their Collection Level by upgrading cards. The higher the rarity upgrade, the more the Collection Level increases. For example, upgrading from Common to Uncommon will increase the Collection Level by a smaller amount than upgrading from Epic to Legendary. Credits and Boosters are interspersed throughout the Collection Level as rewards, but the base cards are the main reward item, so the player increases their owned pool of cards and potential to build interesting decks the higher their Collection Level.

During the primary stages of the Collection Level progress, players are awarded with predefined cards, giving the player the game's starter cards. At this point, the player is onboarding, and designers are looking to keep all players experiencing the same unlocks. From here, the player begins to unlock mystery cards. Cards are classified into different pools, referred to as Series. After the onboarding phase, the player unlocks cards from Series 1 for a set number of Collection Levels. At a certain threshold Collection Level, the player progresses to unlocking Series 2 cards. There are five series in total. The special properties of cards in higher series are generally more tailored to advanced strategic play. With this design approach, designers can keep variety and randomness with the cards that different players own, but also maintain control over the overall potential ownership of certain cards, i.e. designers can know that a player at Collection Level N can only own cards from a specific series.

The method of distribution changes the further into the Collection Level the player reaches. Gacha boxes called Collector's Caches, Collector's Reserves and Spotlight Caches are used to distribute higher series cards. These gacha boxes have the potential to contain currency instead of cards, therefore the distribution of new cards can be further controlled and, in particular, slowed down by the developers.

Battle Pass Progression   *Marvel Snap* includes a Battle Pass, which is referred to as a *Season Pass* within the context of the game. This contains content around a specific theme. The game connects the Season Pass with the common practice of including intrinsic challenges. The game includes several sets of missions which are the main source for Season Pass Xp. These missions unlock over time during a season, controlling the pace at which players can progress through the Season Pass. This timed unlock helps to provide a steady cadence of rewards and helps to push the player toward regular habits of play.

The game includes daily missions which are primarily a source of Credits, but they also serve as the regular recurring source for small amounts of Season Pass Xp. In this sense, the daily missions provide continuous minor incremental progress, and the season-specific missions provide boosts of progress.

Ranks   The recognition for successful play is handled through the rank progression. From winning matches, players earn a specific resource called Cubes. Losing matches causes players to lose Cubes. The Cubes contribute to the player increasing their rank, which provides defined rewards including currency and card variants. Rank progression is tied to the game's seasons (in tandem with the Season Pass), with cosmetic rewards in line with the season's theme available to unlock.

Monetization

The game's premium currency is called Gold, acquired primarily through microtransactions. Due to the free-to-play business model, the game features consistent sources for delivering small amounts of free Gold to the player.

The player can use Gold for various purposes:

- Purchasing card variants which are cosmetic in nature
- Purchasing Credits for Gold, in set amounts
- Daily mission refill
- Special store offers

Purchasing Variants   The player can use Gold to purchase variants of the base cards from the in-game store. The variants have the same functional gameplay properties as the base cards, but simply include alternate artwork for the character they represent. Variants use the same pool of Boosters for upgrading as the base card. Therefore, the benefit of purchasing variants is that the player will gain more opportunities to upgrade with more variants in their possession. Therefore, the player will, on average, increase their Collection Level faster by purchasing and then upgrading variants. Crucially, the player must still play the game to upgrade these variants. There is no complete buy around for acquiring Boosters.

Pinch Point Design   The main pinch point within the game derives from the ability for the player to gain a lot of Boosters directly via the gameplay, but not have enough Credits in order to use the Boosters for card upgrades. Essentially Boosters are given directly from the gameplay in a guaranteed fashion, and as Credits are given for daily challenges and other sources, they are much more limited, so these will run out. The Boosters are also card specific, which also greatly helps the balancing task.

There is also the fast upgrade area within the game's store which allows the player to spend Credits to upgrade cards; essentially a buy-around for the Boosters using Credits (charged at one booster for five Credits). Using this fast upgrade area is appealing to players, as the player receives spikes in their progression without the need for gameplay. However, over extended time with the game, it becomes highly inefficient to use these fast upgrades as Credits are not added to the economy as frequently as Boosters. Players run out of Credits and the overall pinch point is exacerbated.

Daily Mission Refill The player can spend Gold to replenish their daily missions. Daily missions are the main method for the player to acquire Credits. Bearing in mind the pinch point the game creates with Credits running out faster than Boosters, the source for gaining Credits is monetized, albeit in a controlled fashion which requires the player to engage further with the game. This also feeds into the daily play sessions, with players who pay to refill their daily missions being required to engage with the game further on the same day.

Purchasing Credits for Gold Also in line with the pinch point design surrounding Credits, the game gives the player the option to buy Credits with Gold, with limitations on the amount of daily purchases possible. This caters to players who are more willing to spend higher amounts of real-world money on the game.

Battle Pass Monetization The Season Pass is utilized in a standard fashion as a driver for monetization along with long-term retention and engagement. The Season Pass is purchased directly with real-world currency and rewards players with a variety of content, including Credits, Boosters and cosmetic items.

The content of the Season Pass is distributed around a strategy. The main aspect advertised to the player is a new card which is included each season. This new card is unlocked upon purchase of the Season Pass (at the first level), with a variant of the card unlocked at level 50 which the player must work toward. This represents the effective end of the planned content of a single Season Pass. However, the player can continue to progress through the Season Pass levels indefinitely, with Season Cache Gacha Boxes awarded on a continuous loop. These are part of the free rewards. This is a simple solution to a design goal for keeping the game in line with contemporary monetization trends, where games give a solid experience for non-paying players, but an enhanced experience for those who pay. In this case, for non-paying players who are very engaged with the game, they are not punished and can gain many rewards continuously.

The concept of cycling content through the game's economy is observed with the fact that the new cards introduced via the Season Pass are subsequently rolled into the game's other content distribution systems. In this sense, the game charges a premium for the new card when initially added, but as the player progresses, the card becomes (potentially) cheaper to acquire.

There is Gold awarded through the Season Pass, with a small amount for free, and other amounts unlocked for paying players. It is a relatively common practice for games to give players a subsequent season for (almost) free for completing a Battle Pass. This is achieved by way of the game charging premium currency for the Battle Pass and then giving away premium currency on certain reward tiers. However, as *Marvel Snap's* Season Pass is purchased directly with real-world money, the Gold rewards do not feed back into the purchase of subsequent Season Passes. Although one could argue that the barrier to making a purchase is stronger when charged directly with a real-world currency, tracking different player spending and engagement habits, along with the balancing of costing, can be made more difficult if one currency is used over many purposes within a free-to-play title. For example, developers can gauge how much time content is worth to players by the quantity of premium currency dropped for free, that the player spends. This distinction can be a challenge to track. In the context of *Marvel Snap*, considering the uses of Gold for different purposes, this approach can be viable.

Store Bundles   The game includes a number of special offers which can include a variety of different items of content: base cards, variants, currency and cosmetics. These bundles are hand crafted by the game's designers, are typically expensive and placed at eye-line and so are visible initially when the player visits the in-game store. The player must scroll past these expensive bundles to see the regular store content: daily offers of variants, fast upgrading of cards, Credits purchases and microtransactions.

As we can see, *Marvel Snap* is an excellent example of a free-to-play design with clean, concise systems for long-term engagement – as aspirational model for game economy designers.

The Finals

The Finals is a free-to-play first-person shooter game for PC and consoles. The game is themed around the eponymous fictional virtual reality gameshow, with environmental destruction being emphasized within the gameplay.

The game launched with several game modes: a Quickplay mode where players play one off matches, which itself features two different ways to play: Quick Cash and Bank It. Quick Cash involves teams of players fighting to extract two vaults of cash, while Bank It challenges teams to collect cash from vaults and defeated players, depositing sufficient amounts to reach a target. Cash in the context of this game is used as score for matches and is not an in-game currency to be spent directly.

The game's main competitive mode is called Tournaments, which allows players to play in knockout tournaments, both ranked and unranked.

The monetization for *The Finals* is centered fully around the Personalization Strategy, which involves players spending real-world money on cosmetic items, along with a Battle Pass providing engagement and content during seasons.

Progression

The progression for *The Finals* is handled in a method befitting a free-to-play title for console and PC. The system is easy to understand and does not include any convoluted complexities.

Players earn the game's in-game soft currency, called VRs, for playing the game. These are spent to unlock new weapons and equipment to take into matches. There is non-linearity as the player can choose what weapons and equipment to unlock. There is a limit on the number of VRs that the player can have at any one time, so players are forced to spend them. While different players can own different items, due to the limit on VRs, designers can control the average pacing with which players acquire the game's weapons and functional equipment.

Playing matches and successfully using weapons and items earn experience points which are applied to those items, causing them to level up. On each new level, a new cosmetic skin is unlocked for the item.

There is overall Career Progression which acts as the "account level" for the player. At successive levels, a cosmetic item is awarded to the player.

The area of the game tailored to higher levels of engagement is the Tournaments mode, where upon unlocking the Ranked Tournament within this, the player has the chance to progress through different leagues by performing well in tournaments. Cosmetic rewards are integrated into the ranks, with different rewards attained by reaching the leagues, and for finishing seasons within the different leagues.

Collectively, progression awards the player some cosmetic items for free. It is important to complement the monetized content with some free items.

The Store

The store for *The Finals* provides the main way for players to interact with the personalization strategy the game employs. All real-world transactions are carried out to attain the game's hard currency, called Multibucks, which are then spent to acquire cosmetic items (Table 7.1).

The costing table for Multibucks is shown above. The pricing model represents a best practice within contemporary video games. The game follows the five SKU (Stock Keeping Unit) model, with the first (cheapest) SKU setting the value of $1 equal to 100 Multibucks. The four other more expensive SKUs show the extra percentage that the player is gaining, which are modest increases.

It is interesting to highlight the arrangement and user experience that the design of the store adheres to.

Table 7.1   The Costing of Premium Currency in *The Finals*

PRICE (USD)	MULTIBUCKS AMOUNT	PERCENTAGE EXTRA
$4.99	500	0
$9.99	1150	15
$19.99	2400	20
$49.99	6250	25
$99.99	13,000	30

From a design standpoint, the premium cosmetic content is presented to the player via the inventory, via complete lists of cosmetic items pertaining to the different body parts, along with various accessories such as pets, emotes and sprays. The player can view the items and directly purchase and then equip them from these inventory screens.

There is a store screen which is accessed from the game's main menu. This screen takes a selection of the cosmetic items available from the inventory and promotes them to the player. In essence, the store is a featured page of the inventory. This may seem like a simple concept, but the direction of this allows postlaunch monetization to be handled in a systematic way. With this approach, the inventory includes all content which is in the game, and therefore the store forms a promoted subset of these items. The content for the store can also be scheduled via the game's backend systems to appear well in advance of going live.

Placing content into bundles compared to selling standalone items always provides design challenges. For example, if an item exists as standalone or is moved into a bundle at a later stage, it would potentially cannibalize sales of the bundle for players who already own the item. In *The Finals*, the designed bundles all follow a specific theme and naturally only belong in their respective bundles. Within the inventory, items from the bundles appear in their relevant categories, but if the player tries to purchase the item, the game's UI will only allow the player to purchase the bundle. Essentially, an individual purchase is not possible to circumvent the aforementioned design problem.

In terms of the user interface design, items and bundles can be viewed with the same screen design. A standalone item essentially acts as a bundle of one item. This keeps consistency and allows content planning to be easily adapted. This also follows the best practice of trying to avoid bespoke screens and content, which creates unnecessary work and makes design changes much more challenging.

The store includes a seasonal starter bundle. Contemporary live service games must respect their seasonal cycles, and providing an updating entry point to purchasing cosmetic content has been proven to have strong results.

The pricing of cosmetic items typically derives from competitor analysis, profit and loss, and the general cost of creating the items. Although there will be similar items, showing some variation within the prices of the items has been shown to promote stronger sales. The prices of the items involve differences, as does the bundling, where bundles contain a variety of items both in terms of type and quantity.

The Battle Pass

The Finals includes a Battle Pass, offering cosmetic rewards for the player as a long-term engagement and monetization system.

Players progress through the Battle Pass by playing the game, which provides a small but consistent amount of special Battle Pass Xp. The game includes Daily and Weekly Contracts (The game's term for challenges/missions), which provide additional boosts of Battle Pass Xp while assisting with the player's daily and weekly engagement with the game.

The Battle Pass can be purchased for the game's hard currency, Multibucks. Following common practices, the player has two purchase options: the premium Battle Pass costing 1150 Multibucks, or the premium Battle Pass with the first 20 levels unlocked, costing 2400 Multibucks. This second more expensive purchase allows the player to acquire the first 20 items of content instantly without the need for extensive play.

The main cost of the Battle Pass purchase equates to $10, which is the industry standard pricing. The purchase including 20 levels, equates to $20, which essentially provides the player with good value in terms of the content instantly provided to the player. Bear in mind that some reward tiers provide Multibucks, so the player gains a small reduction in the cost of the purchase. Considering the cost of other cosmetics available, the player is instantly gaining an amount of varied cosmetics (about 10 items) for $10; the additional $10 beyond the ten required for purchase.

For players who purchase the Battle Pass and progress through to the final level, they will in total receive 1575 Multibucks, which is sufficient to purchase the Battle Pass of the following season, with an amount left over to put toward other cosmetic items.

It should be evident from the above that *The Finals* is a very good example of the way in which highly skilled product ownership over the monetization and in-game store can result in a successful project.

References

Deconstructor of Fun, "Why Marvel Snap became a hit and for how long will it remain one?", 2022, www.deconstructoroffun.com

Out of Games, "A Guide to Marvel Snap's Season Pass", 2023, https://outof.games/realms/marvel-snap/guides/275-a-guide-to-marvel-snaps-season-pass/

Index

Note: Locators in *italics* represent figures and **bold** indicate tables in the text.

Printed in the United States
by Baker & Taylor Publisher Services